T0222347

Karma-based API on Apple Platforms

Building Privacy Into iOS and macOS Apps

Manuel Carrasco Molina

Apress®

Karma-based API on Apple Platforms: Building Privacy Into iOS and macOS Apps

Manuel Carrasco Molina
Düren, Nordrhein-Westfalen, Germany

ISBN-13 (pbk): 978-1-4842-4290-2   ISBN-13 (electronic): 978-1-4842-4291-9
https://doi.org/10.1007/978-1-4842-4291-9

Managing Director, Apress Media LLC: Welmoed Spahr
Acquisitions Editor: Aaron Black
Development Editor: James Markham
Coordinating Editor: Jessica Vakili

Cover designed by eStudioCalamar

Cover image designed by Freepik (www.freepik.com)

Distributed to the book trade worldwide by Springer Science+Business Media New York, 233 Spring Street, 6th Floor, New York, NY 10013. Phone 1-800-SPRINGER, fax (201) 348-4505, e-mail orders-ny@springer-sbm.com, or visit www.springeronline.com. Apress Media, LLC is a California LLC and the sole member (owner) is Springer Science + Business Media Finance Inc (SSBM Finance Inc). SSBM Finance Inc is a **Delaware** corporation.

For information on translations, please e-mail rights@apress.com, or visit www.apress.com/rights-permissions.

Apress titles may be purchased in bulk for academic, corporate, or promotional use. eBook versions and licenses are also available for most titles. For more information, reference our Print and eBook Bulk Sales web page at www.apress.com/bulk-sales.

Any source code or other supplementary material referenced by the author in this book is available to readers on GitHub via the book's product page, located at www.apress.com/978-1-4842-4290-2. For more detailed information, please visit www.apress.com/source-code.

Printed on acid-free paper

For the men of my life

My dad changed my life by having me realize many small details when he was leaving us.

Steve is for many of us nerds like a common dad. I hope to be one of the crazy ones.

David Servan-Schreiber wrote the most important book I ever read in my life. Read it.

Manfred would be proud of me writing a book: a book, on paper, from me, his digital friend.

It might sound weird to dedicate a book to people I lost, but like I said when my 96-year-old grandma left us, "People you love never really die — they live, inside of you".

Those men left too young, but their time on this planet was absolutely worth every second.

Thanks for building me.

Thanks to you also obviously, the woman of my life. Better than any of the projects I will ever build, we built 4 amazing beings. Thanks for letting me do all those crazy projects those last 20 years of our common life.

I won't be the 2019 version of me without you.

Table of Contents

About the Author

Manuel Carrasco Molina — better known as StuFF mc — started programming with his C64 at age 11 in 1987. He entered professional software development in 1997 and has been developing ever since. He founded the first French podcast about Apple in 2005, and dove into iOS development at the launch of the SDK in 2008. He ran `ObjCGN.com/SwiftConf.com` from 2012 to 2017. He had the privilege of writing Apps with Swift pre-1.0 at Seven Principles from 2014 on. They now run the conference. From 2017 until 2019 Stuff worked at Certgate, a tech firm specializing in security and privacy. In July 2019 he started working for e.GO:Digital as Senior Lead Apple Technologist, building Apps around Mobility. Although he likes Apple a lot, Stuff does prefer the environment and ethics, so let him know if you need him as a regular iOS or macOS Developer or to review a subject like Privacy or Energy Optimization. He also speaks regularly at conferences about those subjects, and will be happy to spread the word at any of your events. He has been involved with the german Green Party since 2011, spent 4 years at the city council and intends to stay at the crossing of politics, technology and activism. He feels a tiny part of the people trying to protect the Hambach Forest and will keep on fighting against big energy corporations for a greener future, which makes him write a greener code.

About the Technical Reviewer

Bruce Wade is a software engineer from British Columbia, Canada. He started software development when he was 16 years old by coding his first website. He went on to study Computer Information Systems at DeVry Institute of Technology in Calgary, then to further enhance his skills he studied Visual & Game Programming at The Art Institute of Vancouver. Over the years he has worked for large corporations as well as several startups. His software experience has led him to utilize many different technologies, including C/C++, Python, Objective-C, Swift, Postgres, and JavaScript. In 2012 he started the company Warply Designed to focus on mobile 2D/3D and OS X development. Aside from hacking out new ideas, he enjoys spending time hiking with his Boxer Rasco, working out, and exploring new adventures.

Acknowledgement

I wouldn't be writing a book on a series of Apple Technologies if Ben "The Sheriff" hadn't challenged me with his Mac in 1999, when I was still a PC guy and Macs were mostly only for designers. He got me in love with the Cupertino-based company. I wouldn't have started Pomcast — the podcast about Apple I started in 2005 — if it wasn't for Vince and HpTroll. From there I got to know and interview a bunch of awesome developers like my very good friends Ken & Glen Aspeslagh (Ecamm); the magnificent Jason Harris (of COTVNC fame); my preferred Bavarian, Ortwin Gentz (FutureTap); as well as many awesome developers you'll find in a screenshot at the end of the chapter about Contacts.

Over the course of my career I've had several mentors. Denis was probably the first one. We don't agree much nowadays, but you were important for me. Frans was the next one and boy was I not surprised when I heard the news back in the day. More recently I've had two CTOs named Andreas whom I always think of, as well as my great colleagues from my two last companies: Seven Principles and Certgate.

Because this book is political and ethical I need to thank my friends Todde, both Michaels, Antje, and Andreas as well as — obviously — the set of amazing people defending the Hambach Forest. It was a smart idea from Clumsy to settle there in 2012. Thanks Tim, thanks Jus, thanks all the Hambis. 2019, Hambi Stays. It was mostly because of those folks that I became vegan, and started to reconsider a lot of the world surrounding us — also capitalism. Of course, without my political involvement for the Greens in Germany I wouldn't be interested in the ethics of IT, so I obviously need to thank them and I will stay at this crossing of technology, politics, and activism. Some of us need to shake up that sometimes so-slow political area.

In a more anonymous way I want to acknowledge all the developers working at Apple on the awesome set of API and Frameworks as well as generally on the beauty and simplicity of the platform. It's fascinating how I haven't been bored at all after 11 years — half of my career as a developer — with UIKit and its brothers and sisters.

Finally, even though I'm not the biggest fan of Android, I have to express my deep respect for Fairtrade, the relatively small company that changed the whole industry. I'm sure Apple wouldn't be what they are without you or Greenpeace, and its "a greener Apple" form back in the day.

Introduction

More than a technical book, this is an ethical book. You'll see a lot of Code samples, discussions about APIs, and screenshots, but it's not my intention to cover every aspect of every API. We'll only look at the parts that are relevant to your privacy and that of users.

The Importance of Privacy

I'm sure there are aspects of other platforms that are better than ours, but everything I read seems to hint at a better respect for my privacy by Apple than, say, Google.

The important part about this is that controlling the whole ecosystem as Apple does is a big part of the challenge about privacy. As we will see, they sadly still rely on other big companies for the servers — which really annoys me — but in terms of software, hardware, and OS, they control it.

Or, at least, for the software, they control the ones they build. Yours, the ones the third-party-developers build, they somehow control via the App Store Review process, at least on iOS.

On the Mac it remains to be seen if the App Store will ever be successful. I had big hopes in 2011 about this, and I would argue now that it would be better for the privacy on your Mac. That being said, over 8 years after the Mac App Store started, it still doesn't have the success some of us thought it would.

I actually removed my own Mac apps from the App Store because I was fighting for months with the review process[1] but for various reasons (one being that many things changed since I left), I'm considering updating some of my apps[2] or starting a new one to give it a chance again.

Let me finish by emphasizing again the importance of controlling the whole chain. I'm a big fan (and a small investor) of Fairphone[3], and I love that this company that is willing to change the electronics world for the better is still successful, while staying a small company in Amsterdam.

The problem with Fairphone is Android. The problem with Android, privacy-wise, is Google. As one friend of mine says:

> *I would miss Photos (I don't want to give Google my photos), iMessage (still no WhatsApp for me), Music, security, AirDrop, how the phone works with my Mac, and so on. I cannot change.*[4]

I too am more confident having my Photos hosted at a company whose business isn't making money with advertising, but rather with over-priced (for a reason) hardware. This cost is partly the price you pay for more privacy. Decide if you want to pay for it or not.

Most likely you're a developer if you bought this book, so you have the advantage of knowing how most things work. You not only make technical decisions, you also make ethical ones. At the end of the day, and if a platform gives you the technical means to do so, you are responsible for dealing with the private data of the user of an app (or indirectly of a framework, for that matter). Some of the decisions you'll need to make, while others have been luckily made by Apple. In this book we will review many details about how you can protect your user's privacy but also what you should keep in mind as a user.

---

[1]And so I moved Disk Alarm to Paddle.com and simply removed the two others.
[2]https://pomcast.biz
[3]https://fairphone.com — As of 2019 still only selling in Europe though.
[4]https://twitter.com/dasdom/status/1029626018196348928

My Privacy.app

To go along with this book, I wrote two sample apps, one for iOS and one for macOS. The idea is to replicate many of the subjects that you can find in Settings ➤ Privacy, with some sample code that illustrates what we speak about in the book.

The iOS version displays a Table View with a list of themes covered throughout the book (Figure 1). I then use some code, which allows me to further develop it in words in the book (Figure 2). The source code for this book is available on GitHub via the book's product page, located at www.apress.com/978-1-4842-4290-2.

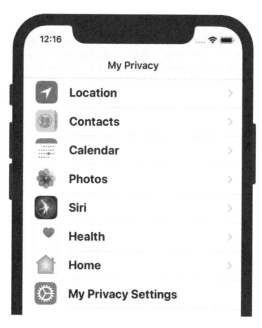

Figure 1. *A set of APIs I'm looking at in the book*

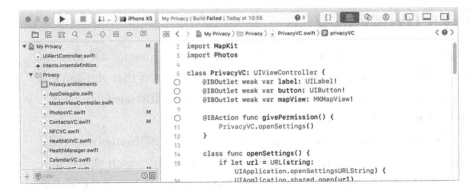

Figure 2. *The iOS Xcode project attached to this book*

The Mac version of the sample app is less detailed than the iOS counterparts but it's also independent (Figure 3). The API, however, is luckily over the years more and more similar to iOS, which makes it convenient.

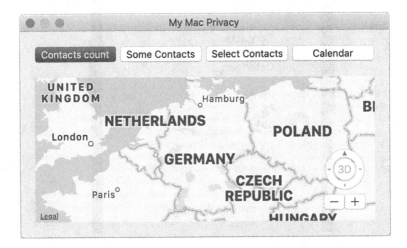

Figure 3. *A simpler Mac app, which goes into some details as well*

Onward

The chapters in this book take a closer look at the different security options given to you by the Apple frameworks, starting with a common part, and then looking into the specifics of subjects like Photos, Location, Calendar.

I hope you enjoy the reading.

CHAPTER 1

Common API Elements

There are a couple of things that are repeatedly the same in the different frameworks that Apple provides.

In this chapter we'll talk about description strings, the alerts shown by the system — not you, the developer —, the possibility a user has to revoke an allowance she previously gave you, and where this all happens in the Settings app.

We'll finish by speaking about the App Store review process, since this is a common subject for the different topics — especially if you're developing for iOS where there's barely another alternative.

Description Strings

The `Info.plist` partly shown in Figure 1-1 is probably something you know. This is where many things like the name of the app or the version is stored. There is a whole list of *privacy*-related keys. This nice looking version (in Xcode) will have a descriptive English text.

Figure 1-1. *The Info.plist and its Photo Library usage description*

© Manuel Carrasco Molina 2019
M. Carrasco Molina, *Karma-based API on Apple Platforms*,
https://doi.org/10.1007/978-1-4842-4291-9_1

Behind the scenes, as you can see in Listing 1-1, this `.plist` is an *XML* file.

Listing 1-1. The XML That Is Used to Present the Previous List

```
<key>NSPhotoLibraryUsageDescription</key>
<string>To visualize your photos on a map</string>
```

If you don't do this, in most cases, you will terribly and sadly crash and see that in your Xcode console. If you're not attached to the debugger, you'll most probably see nothing, so be sure to insert this in your plist.

> *App has crashed because it attempted to access privacy-sensitive data without a usage description. The app's Info.plist must contain a UsageDescription key with a string value explaining to the user how the app uses this data.*

Also, this isn't only necessary for your app to successfully run; it's also an obligation from Apple.

> *Supply a purpose string (sometimes called a usage description string) in your app's Info.plist file that the system can present to a user explaining why your app needs access.*
>
> — Protecting the User's Privacy[1]

Also in this document from Apple you'll find the list of Description Strings keys, but I'll spare you the round trip and list some of it here as well.

- NSBluetoothPeripheralUsageDescription
- NSCalendarsUsageDescription
- NSCameraUsageDescription

---

[1] `https://developer.apple.com/documentation/uikit/core_app/protecting_the_user_s_privacy`

- NSContactsUsageDescription
- NSHealthShareUsageDescription
- NSHealthUpdateUsageDescription
- NSHomeKitUsageDescription
- NSLocationWhenInUseUsageDescription
- NSLocationAlwaysUsageDescription
- NSLocationAlwaysAndWhenInUsageDescription
- NSMicrophoneUsageDescription
- NSMotionUsageDescription
- NSAppleMusicUsageDescription
- NSPhotoLibraryUsageDescription
- NSRemindersUsageDescription
- NSSiriUsageDescription
- NSSpeechRecognitionUsageDescription
- NSVideoSubscriberAccountUsageDescription

Don't be surprised if not all the keys are listed here. I found other ones not listed here. My guess is that Apple doesn't update this document each time they add support for a key.

Authorizations Alerts

Most APIs that are related to privacy on iOS will present a UIAlertController that comes from the system, similar to what is shown in Figure 1-2.

Figure 1-2. *The app called "DetectLocation" will show this alert to the user as soon as the developer uses the corresponding code*

DetectLocation is an app built by the amazing Felix Krause,[2] which inspired me a lot to spend more time in the field of privacy on Apple Platforms.

This kind of system alert is what Steve Jobs meant[3] in 2010 when he said:

> *Before any app can get location data we don't make it a rule that the developers must put up a panel and ask because they might not follow that rule. They call our location services and we put up the panel, saying "this app wants to use your location data, is that OK with you?"*

So, the very first time your app is going to call the code in Listing 1-2, this panel will show up, and you don't get to decide.

Listing 1-2. The Necessary Code for Asking the System for Permission to Access the User's Photo Library

```
PHPhotoLibrary.requestAuthorization { status in
      switch status {
      case .authorized:
```

---

[2]http://krausefx.com/privacy is an amazing resource for checking iOS's privacy.
[3]https://esquire.com/uk/latest-news/a19614236/steve-jobs-warned-us-all-about-the-facebook-data-scandal · https://youtu.be/39iKLwlUqBo?t=83

```
    case .denied:
    case .notDetermined: // User will make a choice
    case .restricted:    // Parental control?
    }
}
```

The answer to that request is in the call-back, and by analyzing the status variable you will know what you can and cannot do.

Revocation of Allowances

If you'd run your code without this authorization you'd see (as a developer) the message in Listing 1-3 in your console.

The previously mentioned authorization status is an enum described in Listing 1-4 (see how CNAuthorizationStatus and PHAuthorizationStatus are the same).

Listing 1-3. The Console Message Appearing When a Developer Forgot to Ask for Permission

```
[Contacts] Access to Contacts denied with error:
Error Domain=CNErrorDomain Code=100 "Access Denied"
This application has not been granted permission to access Contacts.
```

Note In some cases, you won't even have a nice message in the console but instead the app will crash. We'll see that later and it's perfectly fine for Apple to do so. You as a developer forgot to implement something, for which no nice user interface should be displayed. When you develop a framework and a fatal error comes because the user (developer) of your framework has wrongly used it, feel free to crash as well.

Listing 1-4. The Statuses that Are Used in Many APIs, like Contacts

```
public enum CNAuthorizationStatus : Int {
    case notDetermined // User has not made a choice
    case restricted    // Application not authorized
    case denied        // User explicitly denied
    case authorized    // Application is authorized
}
```

Always Check Authorization Status

The problem is that once the user has made a choice (and for example *authorized* the app to access the data), either the user or a system like an MDM[4] might close the door again afterwards.

What it means for you as the developer of an app accessing data is that you should never rest on your laurels, and each time you need to access the data, you should check if you still have the permission to do so.

You won't always crash if you don't do so, but you just won't have access to the data you think you have access to, and I'll let your imagination be filled with a few nils, nulls, NSNulls, and the like.

One technique I use — displayed in Listing 1-5 — is that I check the two statuses, which means I'm either already authorized or it's going to be the first time I ask. These are, as of iOS 12 and macOS 10.14, the only two *good statuses*.

The two others (denied or restricted) aren't much of a great thing for you the developer, so you should display a message (worst case a UIAlertController, best case some graphic with text) telling the user you can't fulfil your task until they (or their administrator) decides whether or not the app is allowed to access the data.

---

[4]Mobile Device Management: A server side architecture that controls the mobile devices in an enterprise, usually. It might also be used for parental control, for example. Speaking of which, the built-in parental controls on Apple devices act the same.

Listing 1-5. The Code You Might Use to Check the Good or Bad News for Being Able to Access the Data

```
if [. authorized, .notDetermined].contains(
    CNContactStore.authorizationStatus(for: .contacts)) {
    // You can proceed and/or ask for the first time
} else {
    // No access until some user/admin action happens
}
```

Apple mentions[5] another approach in the documentation, with the example of capturing Audio or Video:

> *Always test the AVCaptureDevice authorizationStatus(for:) method before setting up a capture session. If the user has not yet granted or denied capture permission, the authorization status is AVAuthorizationStatus.notDetermined. In this case, use the requestAccess(for:completionHandler:) method to tell iOS to prompt the user.*

This is surely an even better approach, but the very important thing to understand is the difference between what you can and cannot do as a programmer. One of the reasons I also ask (`requestAccess`) in the case of `.authorized` is that I've had bad experiences in the past where it said it is authorized, but in fact the question/alert hadn't come yet.

Ask Again

What do you do exactly when the user decides to deny you access? By all means you should display something, where you can't display the actual data (contact, photo, current location, …). But as shown in Figure 1-3,

---

[5]https://developer.apple.com/documentation/avfoundation/cameras_and_media_capture/requesting_authorization_for_media_capture_on_macos

if you want to give your app more of a chance to do something, you can also add a button that will exit the app while leaving a handy "Back" button in the top left corner of the screen, as shown in Figure 1-4.

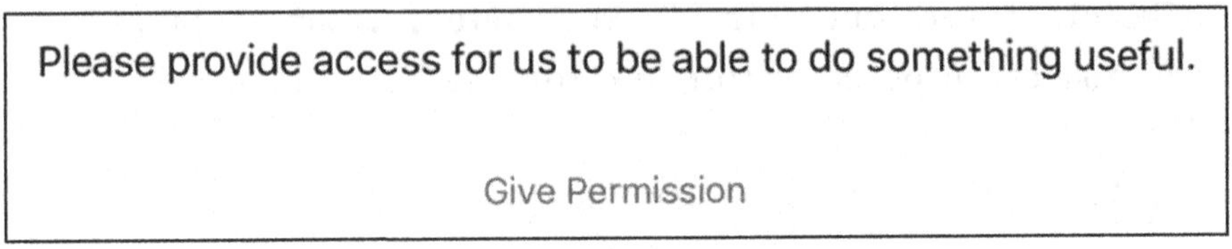

Please provide access for us to be able to do something useful.

Give Permission

Figure 1-3. *Provide a user interface to redirect the user to the privacy settings*

That button (**Give Permission**), when tapped, will call the code in Listing 1-6, which will then display the Settings while having a Back button like in Figure 1-4.

Listing 1-6. Open the iOS Settings at the Right Location

```
@IBAction func givePermission() {
   if let url =
URL(string: UIApplicationOpenSettingsURLString) {
            UIApplication.shared.open(url)
   }
}
```

Note As of now, we'll use the demo app built to demonstrate the different options the API gives us. The app called "My Privacy" reflects many of the user interfaces found in the Settings of your iPhone.

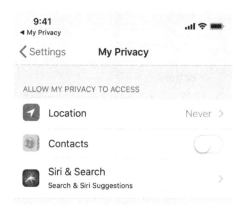

Figure 1-4. *At the top left corner of your iOS Device you'll find the back button*

That *Ask Again* section can't be finished without remembering another quote from that same previously mentioned interview at the D8 Conference in 2010.

> *"Ask them. Ask them every time. Make them tell you to stop asking them if they get tired of you asking them. Let them know precisely what you're going to do with their data."*

— Steve Jobs

All the Apps in the Settings

There are two ways to see the privacy settings of an app. The first, as displayed in Figure 1-5, is by first entering the general Privacy Menu of the Settings app.

At the time of this writing, in iOS 11, 12 or 13, it's the last item of the third section if you don't count the iCloud section, which I'd refer as section 0 because I'm a developer.

Figure 1-5. *The general Privacy section, which lists all apps*

Once you tap on the *Privacy* row you'll see a list of all the services for which Apple has thought about protecting you, as you can see in Figure 1-6, which is the iPad version of the screenshot so you can see the complete list.

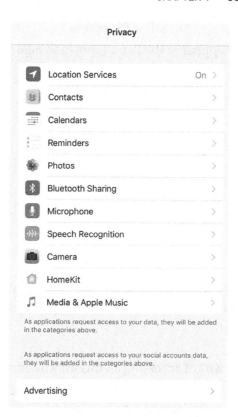

Figure 1-6. *The list of services that can be covered by iOS*

Once you tap, for example, *Contacts,* you'll see a list of apps that are trying to use the Contact API. Figure 1-7 shows what happens when absolutely no apps on your phone have tried to access your contacts yet.

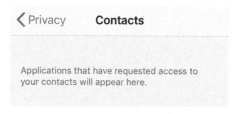

Figure 1-7. *If no applications have requested access to your Contacts database yet, iOS will have nothing to show*

However, once an app has asked for access to, for example, your location, then, it will appear in the list, as shown in Figure 1-8.

Figure 1-8. *Before doing this screenshot we had already started the Calendar app, which, when starting, asks for permission to use our location*

There is another way of accessing all this information, and that's what we show in Figures 1-9 and 1-10. The first time you have a cleanly installed iOS device, the Settings app's Table View stops after *Game Center*, or, if you are a developer, after *Developer*.

The moment you install a third-party app (and by that we also count apps from Apple, e.g., Numbers), you'll see a new (a last) section listing those apps that aren't system apps.

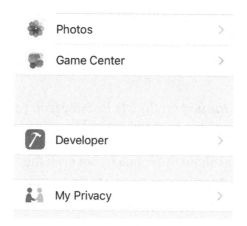

Figure 1-9. *After the Game Center item, potentially a Developer item (which isn't on a normal user's device), if you've already used an API that have a setting to be displayed, or if you have a settings.bundle, you'll see its own section.*

The settings.bundle discussion is out of scope, but it's basically a way for an app to have its own settings menu. It does not have much to do with privacy, although you sure could have privacy-related internal decisions in your app listed here (e.g., reading only some groups of contacts) but nothing API-wise would force you to respect this.

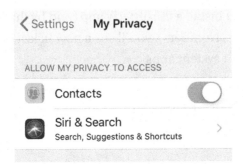

Figure 1-10. *Once tapped on the My Privacy icon (which is my Demo app for the book), you can see I was asked for access to Contacts*

Before I was asked about the contacts, not even the *Siri & Search* menu item would be reachable there, because *My Privacy* wouldn't appear in the list after (in our case) *Developer*.

Settings, General, Reset

By now, if you were to do a simple iOS app and start it the first time, you'd see an authorization request, as we mentioned. Then if you want to test how this System request came about, you'd think you just need to delete the app.

You'll be surprised to not see the system request again and find in the Settings of the app (or in the Privacy section) the same value you once had set.

This is because authorization requests are preserved, much like the keychain elements when you delete an app.

If you want to reset its value and see the system request again, you'll have to reach the screen shown in Figure 1-11, which is in the Settings app under General, Reset and then tap on Reset Location and Privacy.

Figure 1-11. *The only way to see those system alerts again if you need to test your code as a developer or see the question again as a user*

Don't be fooled by the noncoherent text that only speaks about location warnings; this works just fine, for example, with Photo Library permissions.

Review on the App Store

No matter what you program, if you release on the App Store (or in some circumstances on TestFlight[6]), you'll be subject to App Store review.

This might be a pain for the developer, but in most of cases this is a very good thing for the user. If you are reading this book, it probably means you are concerned about privacy, but imagine the number of apps out there that are not concerned at all with that matter.

---

[6]https://developer.apple.com/testflight is Apple's testing platform where you can deploy builds of your app to beta testers or at a larger scale for apps you don't want on the App Store, or to test them before they go on the App Store.

The App Store Review Guidelines[7] not only have a whole section about privacy, they also refer to it in the Kids Category section.

> *You should also pay particular attention to privacy laws around the world relating to the collection of data from children online. Be sure to review the Privacy section of these guidelines for more information.*

I've done an app for kids in the past. It's a pain to have to deal with the privacy, but it's a really good thing.

Reading at least the part on privacy will give you great links to further reading like *Protecting the User's Privacy*.[8] There are also some parts that I'd like to highlight here. The first one corresponds to a subject I touched on already in a previous section.

> *Explain its data retention/deletion policies and describe how a user can revoke consent and/or request deletion of the user's data.*

It's also interesting to see a part about GDPR[9] there. Although this is only for your users residing in the European Union, it's a good idea — and if fact what Apple does — to practically apply GDPR to all your users, no matter where they live.

There is a bit about always trying to find an alternative experience, which I really like:

> *Where possible, provide alternative solutions for users who don't grant consent. For example, if a user declines to share Location, offer the ability to manually enter an address.*

Sure, it means more work for a developer — and a designer — but it also means more potential customers for your app. I'm the example of

---

[7]https://developer.apple.com/app-store/review/guidelines
[8]https://developer.apple.com/documentation/uikit/core_app/
 protecting_the_user_s_privacy
[9]https://www.eugdpr.org

the consumer who rejects most apps that want access to my Contacts database. If you provide me a way to save contacts in-app, without having access to my Contacts, then I'll be a happy customer of your app.

If, on the other hand, you don't provide that option and simply don't allow me to use your app, there's a good chance I'll not only not use the app but also speak badly about it around me. It's a good idea to spare some bad publicity by working a little bit harder.

Some of the paragraphs are more explicit than others:

> *(vi) Developers that use their apps to surreptitiously discover passwords or other private data will be removed from the Developer Program.*

This is the whole point of doing an app review by humans: those things can't really be checked by a computer — at least at this state of artificial intelligence.

Some of the points you really hope — as a privacy evangelist — will evolve, because they're not strict enough.

> *Data collected from apps may only be shared with third parties to improve the app or serve advertising.*

Time will tell if Apple will in the future completely ban advertising from its platform. Some parts of this Guideline are so impossible to check that you wonder if they only wanted to fill the paper.

> *Do not use information from Contacts, Photos, or other APIs that access user data to build a contact database for your own use or for sale/distribution to third parties, and don't collect information about which other apps are installed on a user's device for the purposes of analytics or advertising/marketing.*

I don't think there's a way to check what a company does with your data, once it's in their hands. The traceability of your data is very complicated. This is also why I recommend trying to use an e-mail scheme like, for example, mail+website@example.com[10] so you can trace that website where you gave your mail@example.com e-mail address.

Conclusion

Learning a new language like Italian is easier if you already speak French and Spanish. Learning Swift is easier if you know C or Ruby already.

Learning a new Privacy-related API is very similar, since the concepts barely change. Most of the APIs use the concept of the Authorization enum with four values, and what really does change is the kind of access you want.

We'll see later, for example, that a nuance was introduced a few years ago between knowing your location all the time or only when the app is in the foreground.

Privacy evangelists like me will probably want to have even more fine-grained control, but I also understand that I don't want the privacy authorizations to be too much in the way of the user.

This is really a big challenge; and never forget that if some of the privacy that Apple requires isn't enough for you, you are welcome to add a bit more fine grain. The problem with it is the exact same problem as with anything that is voluntary: there are barely any controls to ensure that you did it the right way.

If, on the contrary, you think Apple does too much about privacy, I'm afraid you are out of luck. For Apple, the user will always be a priority rather than the developer, and this is a good thing in my opinion.

---

[10]Most e-mail providers will allow use of the + sign and the e-mail will land at the e-mail address before the + sign. This allows you to identify who gave your address or who got it stolen. Sadly, some apps and websites don't allow this usage. You should always accept "+" as a symbol pre-@ in the e-mail. Whether this is actually supported by the user's e-mail provider shouldn't be your concern.

CHAPTER 2

Photos and Camera

This chapter discusses the different options a developer and user have to access the photo library as well as use the camera. Because a picture also carries a lot of Metadata, we'll spend some time looking at those.

We will look at the out-of-process picker as well as analyze which information is in the dictionary received for each picture.

The second part of this chapter looks at technologies like Photos extensions, and facial recognition.

Full Access and Geolocation

From a user's perspective, the *"would like to access your Photos"* request should be alarming.

Literally, it should be shown with a big red stop sign. Depending on what you answer — and what the developer asked — it means you're giving away all your images.

If the `PHPhotoLibrary.requestAuthorization` is accepted by the user, or postaccepted afterward in the settings, the developer can do a lot.

Of course, they can display the images, change them however they want, even upload them, but the Photo Library (meaning the photos in your Photos.app) doesn't only contain raw JPEG/HEIFF data.

© Manuel Carrasco Molina 2019
M. Carrasco Molina, *Karma-based API on Apple Platforms*,
https://doi.org/10.1007/978-1-4842-4291-9_2

A Picture Worth 1000 Metadata

Metadata is added information. A picture often refers to it more specifically as EXIF (exchangeable image file format),[1] and the example shown in Figure 2-1 displays the location where the pictures where taken.

We found 5 assets

Figure 2-1. *Using the geolocation part of pictures you take on your iPhone*

If you know a little bit about how MapKit and PHAsset work, it's trivial to write the Model in Listing 2-1.

In a nutshell, it uses the location (and to some extent, creationDate) that a picture has. The latter will always be present, whereas the

---

[1]Exchangeable image file format: https://en.wikipedia.org/wiki/Exif

geolocation will only be present if you accepted the authorization (yes, again) the first time you used the camera on your device. You can also turn it off in the Privacy/Location Services of your app, as shown in Figure 2-2.

Figure 2-2. *Not showing "Never"? Your pictures are geotagged*

Convenience vs. Privacy

Maybe you've heard about convenience over security. This is the same. It's more of an advantage that my pictures are geotagged, or face recognized. Remember when we used to have a folder called Spain, another one called Steve, and so on? Computers — in some cases more specifically, machine learning — are taking away a lot of the boring work (or did you enjoy creating those folders and moving files in them) but it's important to think about to which app you'd want to grant that freedom.

Listing 2-1. Adding This Image to the Map Is Enough for it to Appear Placed and with the Date as a Title

```
class Image: NSObject, MKAnnotation {
    var asset: PHAsset
    var dateFormatter: DateFormatter

    init(asset: PHAsset, dateFormatter: DateFormatter) {
        self.asset = asset
        self.dateFormatter = dateFormatter
        super.init()
    }
```

```
var coordinate: CLLocationCoordinate2D {
    get { return asset.location!.coordinate }
}

var title: String? {
    get { return
            dateFormatter.string(from:
                                 asset.creationDate!)}
}
}
```

Pick Only One or a Few Pictures

There are many cases where all you want is the ability for an app to browse your pictures while not having control of them. Imagine, for example, being able to select an avatar for your preferred social network. If this social network understands anything about privacy, it shouldn't ask for full control of your Photo Library.

Instead, it could use the UIImagePickerController[2] API, which is demonstrated in Listing 2-2, by clicking **Pick** in the Demo App, instead of **Allow**. I'm also showing you what I mean with those buttons in Figure 2-3.

Listing 2-2. The User Decides Which Picture They Give to the App

```
let picker = UIImagePickerController() // Out of Process!
picker.sourceType = .photoLibrary // or .camera
picker.delegate = self
present(picker, animated: true) { }
```

---

[2]This API is in UIKit, so you don't even need to add/import the Photos framework to use it.

```
func imagePickerController(
    _ picker: UIImagePickerController,
    didFinishPickingMediaWithInfo info:
            [UIImagePickerController.InfoKey: Any]) {
    print(info)
}
```

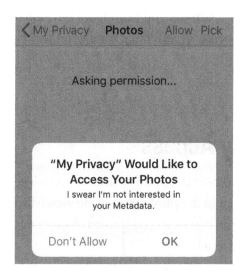

Figure 2-3. *The user just tapped Allow, which uses the requestAuthorization API and thus shows the corresponding description from the Info.plist.*

If the user instead taps *Pick,* they won't see the system request because the out of process picker is used.

Be aware that you need to use NSPhotoLibraryUsageDescription in your Info.plist, as mentioned in Chapter 1.

The App Store Review Guidelines[3] encourage their usage, but they are sadly not yet available for each API.

---

[3]https://developer.apple.com/app-store/review/guidelines

Where possible, use the out-of-process picker or a share sheet rather than requesting full access to protected resources like Photos or Contacts.

Note Before iOS 11, the image picker wasn't out-of-process. It means it was showing the same "Would like" alert seen in Figures 2-3 and 2-4. This book assumes you're at least developing for iOS 11, at best for iOS 12 or even 13; but if you develop for an earlier iOS, don't be surprised.[4]

Camera-Only Access

Once you understand how the picker works, it's relatively trivial to use it for the camera instead of the photo library. Be aware though that these are two different permissions, so you'll need NSCameraUsageDescription instead and .camera as a type.

The first one goes in the info.plist and the second is the only line you need to change from Listing 2-2.

---

[4]The general recommendation for a developer working with Apple technologies is to support the "-1" Operating System. It means if iOS 13 is the current system, you should support iOS 12. Of course, if you have already an app supporting iOS 10 you don't need to remove its support, but remember that users can always access old versions of your app. My personal decision, whenever I develop a new app, is to support only the current OS, even if I release the app the day the OS is released. It allows you to use the latest APIs and Apple will be more likely to feature you. One could argue that it's ethically better to support old devices but you also must think about the number of devices you'd need to test.

The call-back function `imagePickerController` is the same, since at the end of the day you'll get an image the same way as if you selected it.

Figure 2-4 shows the kind of system request access that comes after the camera UI has been presented. Although it's the same picker, it makes sense for it to ask for permission for the camera that will produce a picture the app will have access to. But more importantly, it will save this image to your library, so at the bare minimum it would need write-only access. The `.photolibrary` version of this code will make it clear to the user that the app will have access to whatever picture they select.

Figure 2-4. *First the user interface appears and then the question is asked*

The weird part about this mechanism of first showing the UI and then asking is that if the user says Don't Allow, the camera interface stays but the picture is obviously black. If you can see the log, you'll see:

```
This app is not authorized to use Back Dual Camera.
```

This is on my iPhone X. If you change to the front camera, you'll see a similar message about the front camera. As you know by now, I can't ask the user again (as a developer), so it's only when this user goes into the settings and moves the switch of *Allow My Privacy to Access Camera* to ON that it'll work again.

It's easy to complain, but that's without remembering that such view controllers provided by Apple are simplifications of usage of another API alternative. They are really useful in many ways and spare you a lot of development time. If you need more control, though, there's always a way to reconstruct those UIs in a more custom manner for your app.

Not for Your Simulator Yet

I like to work in the simulator because it's convenient. At one point, sure, you do have to intensively test on the device, but in most cases, it then works as expected. The simulator doesn't simulate everything, though. Camera support, much like Bluetooth support, is something the simulator doesn't have.[5]

Inside That `info` Dictionary

First of all, please note that we will use the newly introduced `UIImagePickerController.InfoKey` that arrived with Swift 4.2.

In the past, for code written with Xcode up until 9.4.1 I'd have referred to string constants like `UIImagePickerControllerImageURL`, but nowadays we'll simply use the shorter version because the signature of `didFinishPickingMediaWithInfo` isn't using `[String:Any]` anymore.

---

[5]Or doesn't have anymore, in the case of Bluetooth. The first iterations of Core Bluetooth worked in the simulator, using the Mac's Bluetooth. Camera Support should work with the Mac Camera as well, so go ahead and write about it at `https://feedbackassistant.apple.com`.

So instead of info[UIImagePickerControllerImageURL], we now use info[.imageURL]. There are different ways to access this picture now and I'll refer to some.

.imageURL
file:///path/to/F54AF01F-C12F-4DE9-9266-06D2DD799C05.jpeg

This is a direct file path to an image file. You use this with any API able to use a file URL: for example, Data(contentsOf: url) or a better (async) version of it. However, this isn't a very useful example because you'll see a way to have a UIImage and from there you could simply use pngData() or jpegData(compressionQuality:).

.phAsset

Enter the wonders of PHAsset and use any of its properties, like .location for example.

Note that these *wonders* can only be entered if you previously have been given access to the library. I know it kind of defies the purpose of the picker, so I wrote a bug report about it. It's also confusing because the old UIImagePickerControllerReferenceURL, which we're not supposed to use anymore, will still give an **assets-library://** URL…

.originalImage
<UIImage: 0x6040002a79e0>
  size {4288, 2848} orientation 0 scale 1.000000

These are probably the most used cases. In an app, as a developer, you either want the UIImage directly or its *data*, in case you want to upload it to your server.

Note that I'm **not** saying you should upload an image that belongs to a user to your server. The technical reality, though, is that as soon as the user gave access to this picture, the developer can't be stopped from doing so.

Also, check if there's an .editedImage before using the original one. Be aware that this will only work if you specified .allowsEditing = true.

Export Without Location?

For whatever reason, Apple seems to think it's perfectly fine to let the GPS information of a photo be shared on iOS, whereas they give the user of the Photos app on the Mac that decision (Figure 2-5).

It's on by default but should you uncheck it, that information will not only be removed before the export, it will also be respected by other APIs.

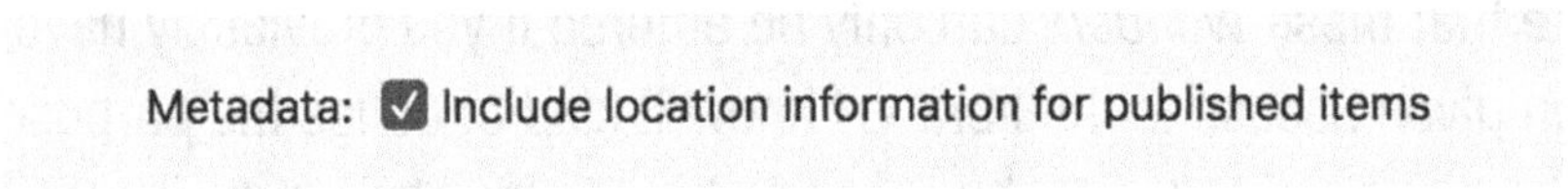

Metadata: ☑ Include location information for published items

Figure 2-5.   In the Photos.app on your Mac, you can choose not to export the location (GPS) information. On iOS it will — if there's any — always be exported.

Write-Only Access

If your app doesn't need to get access to the user's library but would still like to save an image (e.g., downloaded from the web or built into the app) to her Camera Roll,[6] you can use the code in Listing 2-3. You can tell that

---

[6]When used on an iOS device without a camera, this method adds the image to the Saved Photos album rather than to the Camera Roll album.

code must be pretty old, since it's still a C function. In fact it's been there since iOS 2.0, which is an interesting way for Apple to refer to iPhone OS 2.0 — the first SDK available to developers not working at Apple.[7]

Listing 2-3. This Simple Function, in Conjuction with an Info.Plist Addition, Will Allow You to Save an Image to the User's Camera Roll

```
let image = #imageLiteral(resourceName: "icon-photos")
// or
let image = UIImage(named: "icon-photos")

UIImageWriteToSavedPhotosAlbum(image, nil, nil, nil)
```

Note three usages of `nil`? I'll let you dig into the documentation and discover why I didn't need it in my example.

Be aware that this book was mostly finished when Apple announced SwiftUI, which anyways is relatively new and fragile. It means all the code in this book is written with general UIKit like it's been done since 2008. This might change slowly, starting with the broader usage of Xcode 11, but it seems that SwiftUI will follow the same fragility that Swift had back in 2014…

The `#imageLiteral` usage in Xcode will show a 🖾 placeholder which might be what you want or not. On the iPad (Swift Playgrounds), it at least shows a little preview of the image, not a generic icon.

---

[7]https://en.wikipedia.org/wiki/IOS_version_history. The term iOS was only coined when iOS 4 arrived. The original iPad was running iPhone OS 3.2 in 2010, which wasn't running on iPhone or iPod touch, and iOS 4.0 and 4.1 weren't running on iPad. Finally, since iOS 4.2, the operating system is the same on both device types. Or not, since Apple now calls the OS running on iPad "iPadOS," since June 2019. Oh, irony… This is more of a marketing than a technical term, though.

To be able to use this function, you need to either have the previously mentioned `NSPhotoLibraryUsageDescription` or the `NSPhotoLibraryAdd UsageDescription` key in your `Info.plist`.

If you only have the latter, your Privacy settings will look like Figure 2-6. If you have the former, because it implies Read and Write you won't see it and it's enough.

If you'd like to give the user the choice between *Add Only* and both *Read and Write* (as well as *Never*, like always) you can use both keys and then it will look like Figure 2-7.

Figure 2-6. *Your app might only need to add photos*

Sadly there's no Read Only, which isn't ideal. I think Apple is itself restricted by its mechanism of using Enums (or constants) for every state, where in this case it would probably make more sense to have a Boolean for read and one for write.

Figure 2-7. *You can give more fine-grained permissions to your user*

Like with all the topics I'm going to cover, you could dream of giving access to only certain albums or certain metadata, but I understand Apple must make usability choices and might come up with a solution in a few years.

Note Whenever I'm unhappy about the current situation of iOS, I think about Copy and Paste. It took Apple many years to come up with a solution that didn't seem to be so complicated to implement. As someone who has built a framework as part of my day job, though, I know that internal decisions aren't always as simple as they look from the outside.

That previous function `UIImageWriteToSavedPhotosAlbum` might not please you a lot, especially if you must have a call-back. A more modern (but more complicated) version of it could be what is shown in Listing 2-4.

It uses the status described in Chapter 1, which we do not check here because we want to focus on the call-back received when performing the change.

Listing 2-4. This Is the Way You Can Combine a requestAuthorization and a Call-Back

```
PHPhotoLibrary.requestAuthorization { (status) in
    // You should obviously check that status!

    PHPhotoLibrary.shared().performChanges({
        PHAssetChangeRequest.creationRequestForAsset
                        (from: image)
    }, completionHandler: { (success, error) in
        // check success and optionally error.
    })
}
```

The problem here is that the code in Listing 2-4 will ask for full access, not only "creation" access, since we requestAuthorization.

Photos App Wants Access to Your Photo?

Not actually. What you see in Figure 2-8 is a Photos extension that I built in my own "My Mac Privacy"[8] app. Whenever the user wants to create something with this for the first time, it will ask for access.

Remember, in this case it's not the Photos app from Apple accessing your picture but this app (or its database or API) providing those Photos to your app.

Figure 2-8. *The warning the system shows you the first time you want to create a project with this extension*

From a privacy perspective it's another deal, because you (the developer) could do anything with those pictures.

The result of this is that your app will be listed in the System Preferences under *Security & Privacy — Privacy — Photos,* as shown in Figure 2-9.

---

[8]This is the Mac Version of "My Privacy", our Demo app.

Figure 2-9. *This decision is persisted in the system preferences of your Mac, and you can then decide to remove the permission.*

Because the user can change their mind later, if your app/extension tries to access photos again you'll see the error in Figure 2-10, which has a beautiful *Open Privacy Settings* button.

That in itself is nice, but the problem is that tapping that button only opens the System Preferences. Apple has fixed it in the latest macOS Catalina 10.15 beta 4 (Build 19A512f) but this was true in macOS 10.13 and is still true in macOS Mojave 10.14.6 (Build 18G84).[9]

---

[9]Feel free to duplicate my radar at www.openradar.me/43240627 if you want it to be fixed in a version prior to 10.15 but even though my report says "Recent Similar Reports: Less than 10", because it also says "Resolution: Open" I imagine Apple will only fix this in 10.15, which is fair enough.

Figure 2-10. *Don't be surprised to see this error if the user has revoked an access*

Since macOS 10.14 Mojave it goes even further because luckily, finally any app (even such a System/Apple app like QuickTime) needs access to the camera and the microphone from the user. Sure, on iOS, it has been like that for many years, but on the Mac it just arrived. And then macOS 10.15 Catalina goes even further in asking permission to other folders.

Facial Recognition with Vision

"We're privacy oriented" is what Apple says at the beginning of the 2018 WWDC session about *Object Tracking in Vision.*[10]

The Problem here is that it's the **only time** they mention it. I'm not sure what they mean except that the processing is on-device, but it doesn't mean the third-party developer isn't storing a representation of this information in the cloud. The only thing that Vision asks a user for is access to the camera or Photo Roll, and it's left to the developer to tell the user it's going to use facial (or else) recognition.

I'd personally prefer something warning the user that Vision is going to be used, because used in the wrong hands this amazing framework could potentially put certain lives in danger.

---

[10]https://developer.apple.com/videos/play/wwdc2018/716

That Amazing TrueDepth Camera

The newly introduced iPhone X in 2017 brought a technology that will surely be available on more and more Apple devices in the future. All three new devices from 2018 (XS, XS Max, XR) have the camera as well. The iPad Pro has it also since 2018.

It not only has a regular camera but (mostly in order to be used by FaceID[11]) it has a special kind of camera that, combined with a Dot Projector, will read 30,000 dots projected on your face.

It's fascinating technology and such an easy API, which Apple demonstrated at the 2018 WWDC,[12] but it also begs the privacy question.

Sure, that information (FaceID at least) is in the secure-enclave, but do I want at all as a user to have my face identified now, even in 3D?

This is another level of privacy, and who knows what kind of technologies will arrive in the future that can potentially be used to make us more and more transparent.

My point is that as long as there's a big enough hint to the user what an app is doing, I'm fine.

Those hints, though, must come from the system, and right now, same as with Vision, there's no hint that this amazing set of camera and sensor is being used (except the global use of the camera).

That last bit is important, though. As far as I could find by looking at the code samples in this WWDC session, and looking on the API, it's all based on AVFoundation, which makes sense. It means it uses AVCaptureDevice.authorizationStatus and .requestAccess. That means that even if you wouldn't show the user but use the TrueDepth

---

[11]https://apple.com/iphone-xs/face-id really shows the complexity of the notch. Never in the past was there so much video-related sensing in an Apple Device.

[12]https://developer.apple.com/videos/play/wwdc2018/503

Camera for, say, a game where your hand would control a ball depending on where you hand is (easier though weirder would be your face with the Vision API), that would still require access to the camera.

That reminds me that it doesn't matter which camera you are using, and what kind of camera it is. This whole set of cameras and projectors will be very useful in the future, and it would be inconvenient if a different authorization was requested for every kind of camera.

What would be great, though, would be an indication somewhere that a camera is being used, at least when it's not obvious that it's on screen.

Conclusion

As with some other privacy-related fields, the camera and the photo library don't only imply your own privacy. It's a tough decision you are making for other people (and yourself) because it would be very complicated if you'd have to ask every single person.

Getting access to your photos in itself isn't the biggest problem. It's the analyzing of those pictures that is a problem. Figure 2-11 shows both the amazingness of the Photos app as well as the dangerousness.

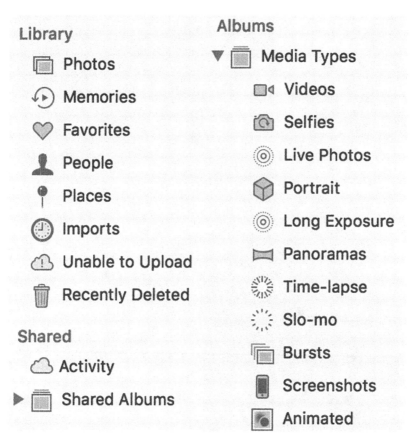

Figure 2-11. *Each one of these items in your Photos library is potentially a violation of your privacy*

I love this app and I love that it crawls my Photos during the night, but it's because I trust Apple to do the right thing.

Whenever an app wants to access to your pictures, consider the kind of information that you potentially have in them.

CHAPTER 3

Location and MapKit

This is what I consider as the most crucial information. It's in many places other than the Location and MapKit framework themselves.

This chapter starts by explaining how the location is gotten at all from iOS. Then it gets deeper about the User location and generally the asynchronousness of it.

We'll also look at the difference between an app having access to your location at any time (that is, in the background) or only when you app is running in the foreground. Bear in mind, though, that foreground doesn't necessarily mean your app is displayed on the screen.[1]

---

[1]But discussing this is out of scope. There's this thing called the Internet where you can find some information about that subject. Alternatively, read another book on the subject.

© Manuel Carrasco Molina 2019
M. Carrasco Molina, *Karma-based API on Apple Platforms*,
https://doi.org/10.1007/978-1-4842-4291-9_3

What is Location on iOS?

Getting a GPS position solely via satellite like regular GPS works takes time. It's because it needs to get answers from several satellites and if you've read about the kind of latency that satellite-based Internet has, you'll know there's a challenge to be solved.

Acquiring the exact location takes an original time called *Time to First Fix*, which can take a while.[2]

Instead, the iPhone uses a technology called Assisted GPS, which uses cellular towers to give you a position. It's less precise, but pretty much instantaneous. Between those two accuracies the iPhone also uses the Wi-Fi router it finds, which are referenced in a database together with their coordinates.

The other problem with GPS is that the signal won't get inside buildings or in a forest,[3] so it's not only a question of speed.

That accuracy translates into `CLLocationAccuracy` when the system reports it has found a position. Possible values are:

- ThreeKilometers

- Kilometer

- HundredMeters

- NearestTenMeters

- Best

- BestForNavigation

---

[2]One of the early Betas of iOS 12 had this terrible bug where only regular GPS would work. The result was having to wait forever for navigation to become useful.

[3]Which in turn will have a hard time with Geo-Location at all anyway because neither cell towers nor Wi-Fi are usually in a forest. If they are, move along; find a real forest.

Except for the last one, those values are self-explanatory. Let's look at what Apple's documentation says for Best for navigation.

The highest possible accuracy that uses additional sensor data to facilitate navigation apps.

There's a property called `desiredAccuracy`, which you should set if you don't need the standard Best (iOS/macOS) or 100m (watchOS). The less accurate, the faster it is and *the less power it consumes*. Be an environmental hero if you can and save power, and so the planet.

Note There's neither a way for the user to select this accuracy nor a way to tell what an app requires. It would probably be a terrible UI and a few more edge cases for a developer, but feel free to make a suggestion to Apple[4] about any of those privacy concerns.

User Location

Core Location and MapKit are two frameworks that cooperate with each other in various means.

The first time you start the Maps app you'll see the authorization asked in Figure 3-1. We'll see in a bit why that is, but maybe you can already discover from the screenshot that even though I didn't give it access, the map is already centered in Germany.

---

[4]`https://bugreport.apple.com` doesn't exist anymore since June 2019. Instead, `https://developer.apple.com/bug-reporting` is where you can express you concerns.

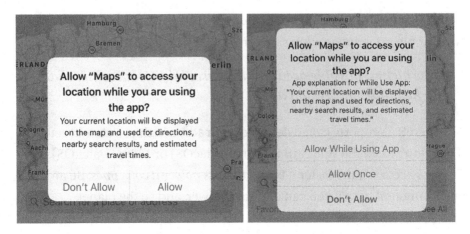

Figure 3-1. *Maps also asks for permission the first time you start it.*
We will see later why this is different on iOS 13 (Right).

Apple doesn't really communicate how it does that, and if we trust
them that they don't have my exact location yet, we can only guess that
they use my IP address, which reveals that I must be in Germany.

On one side, it's a privacy constraint. On the other, the whole Internet
is based on it[5] to display location-based information that doesn't need a
precise location.

Whenever you want to display the well-known blue dot that displays
the user's current location, you can request so with a simple property on
an MKMapView element.

This property is also available via Interface Builder, as shown in
Figure 3-2.

---

[5]In fact, if you don't live in the USA, Apple's own website will offer you to go to
your country/language's website when you go to apple.com

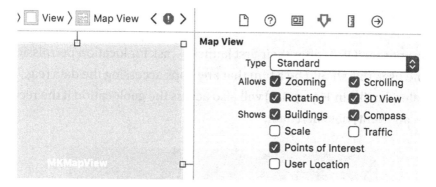

Figure 3-2. *You can set* `.showsUserLocation` *in code or in Xcode*

Nothing Happens?

First, be patient. Wait. As we mentioned, getting a position takes time. If you're lucky it will only take a couple of milliseconds, but it can't be instantaneous. The asynchronous call-back, as shown in Listing 3-1, will then be called when the fix has been found.

Don't forget, you need to set the `delegate` on the MapView for it to know where to expect the method to be found.

If you check `userLocation.isUpdating` you'll know if you still need to wait. The problem is that if you forgot (as a developer) to implement the authorization request, you won't see an error in your Xcode console — or even a crash or any hint — but nothing will happen.

Listing 3-1. The Asynchronous Call That Is Called on the Delegate

```
func mapView(_          mapView    : MKMapView,
         didUpdate userLocation: MKUserLocation) {

  mapView.setCenter(userLocation.coordinate,
                                      animated: true)
}
```

When You First Start an App

Many apps on iOS — after their first launch — ask for location permission.
For the user, this should be a hint that any apps accessing the data (e.g., of
the calendar like in Figure 3-3) will also access the geolocation if the record
(here, an Event) has such data.

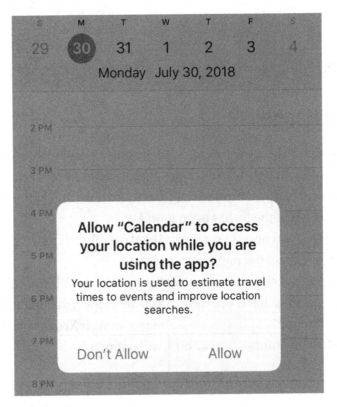

Figure 3-3. *When first launching the Calendar.app, you'll be
prompted about the usage of your location. Should you accept, this
information will be found in events. This is for iOS 12. If you are
running iOS 13, you will have 3 options similarly to Figure 3-1.*

Always or When in Use?

We've seen that most authorization requests are the same and respond with a few different statuses like authorized or denied.

Core Location is a bit different, though, because there are two different levels of using your location. In iOS 13 we'll see that there is the concept of "Allow Once", so one could argue it's three levels.

Depending on the call in your code, a different system UI will be shown. In Listing 3-2 we show an example of a controller (e.g., a UIViewController on iOS) having this code as part of the class.

Listing 3-2. How Often Does Your App Need to Know the User Location

```
let locationManager = CLLocationManager()

func viewDidAppear(_ animated: Bool) {
  // ...
  locationManager.requestWhenInUseAuthorization()
  // or
  locationManager.requestAlwaysAuthorization()
```

Note that both of these methods require usage descriptions inside Info.plist in order for them to work. Otherwise you get a message printing in the output but don't actually get the prompt.

This is effectively a choice only on iOS. On macOS[6] your only choice is *Always*, but there it kind of makes sense because there's usually more than one app on the screen.

---

[6]And in very ancient versions of iOS, but this book assumes you are at least developing for iOS 11 and for any 64-bit device from Apple.

That means that iPad Apps running on the Mac (Refered since macOS 10.15 and iOS 13 as *UIKit for Mac* or *Catalyst*) should only think about it for iOS. When they run on a Mac, it doesn't matter if whenInUse was called, it will always be *Always*.

On the contrary, on tvOS and watchOS, there's no *Always*. Specifically on watchOS if your app has a Complication it is InUse anyways and for obvious battery reasons Apple doesn't want your watch to constantly get locations in the background. This is why you'll have a hard time finding an API that can use a background location call on those platforms.

That being said please note that *When in Use* doesn't imply the app is the front most, the one the user sees. All it means is that it's running, but it could be running in the background. The *Always* authorisation though will restart your process whenever a location is sent from the system, even if the app was killed by the user, or crashed.

Provisional Always Authorization

I'll go into more details when speaking about elevation of privileges but for now remember that since iOS 13 there is no way to directly ask Always.

You can still call requestAlways but the user will see the same prompt as if you'd ask WhenInUse. The system will however remember / know you (as the developer) wanted to have Always and gather the location informations in the background.

It won't however deliver those to you until the user is later prompted by the system to *Change to Always Allow* or *Keep only while using*. In effect Apple is enforcing the elevation of privilege, which is a very elegant way of doing it.

Whatever the user then chooses, the Provisional Always Authorization period then ends. It means as of now (and this is your only chance) the app will have either one of the options. The user can however — as usual with permissions — change her mind about this at a later time in the Settings App on iOS.

If you need a reason to explain your boss / company why your app shouldn't support iOS 12 anymore very soon (or shouldn't at all if you release the App after September 2019), this is a good reason.

Another one unrelated to Location are the new modal view controllers which you'll see in the Chapter about Health.

With Great Power...

Ask yourself a couple of questions. As a developer, do you really need access to the location of your user when they are not using the app? As a user, do you really want this app to know where you are — all the time, every time?

Also, as a side note, think about the battery consumption. We as developers are also environmentally responsible for our acts, and the more often hardware is used (sensors), the faster the battery gets drained.

Core Location

MapKit only arrived in 2009, with iPhone OS 3.0. Core Location though, which is the nongraphical version, was there from day one in iPhone OS 2.0.[7]

By nongraphical I mean that Core Location doesn't display a map like MapKit does but instead gets the coordinate of a user.

---

[7]Remember that iPhone OS 1 didn't have an SDK, so it wasn't possible to develop, even though some did reverse engineer and made some nice first apps. Also remember the term iOS was only coined with version 4 of the OS, which is why I refer to those previous versions as iPhone OS. Ironically the iOS running on iPad since iOS 13 is called iPadOS.

What Is a Coordinate?

Let's step back and take a broader picture, because a coordinate really isn't hard to understand — it's essentially a latitude and longitude as you'd expect from a world map.

More interesting though is a CLLocation object. This is, for example, a property of a PHAsset, which allows you to locate a picture you took.

A location object doesn't only have a coordinate but it has also an altitude, because really only flat-earthers probably also think there's no such thing as mountains and valleys.[8]

Remember we spoke about accuracy at the beginning of this chapter? Guess what: a location object doesn't have only one, but two. One is vertical, the other one horizontal.

It also has a course and a speed, which combined together can let you know if a picture was taken in an airplane or not moving at all.[9]

On iOS you can even know in which floor of the building you are in the picture (or any other object having a coordinate) was!

Geocoding and Decoding

Let's face it: if I tell you I'm at this place in Figure 3-4 while writing this chapter, you'll have a hard time finding where I was — if not for that hint in the picture.

---

[8]They also believe there are no such thing as satellites, so I guess that location thing is a myth. https://therichest.com/shocking/15-stupid-things-flat-earthers-believe-are-true

[9]There are a lot of the things in this book inspired from the amazing research Felix Krause did. You should check out https://krausefx.com/privacy.

Figure 3-4. *This is where I am when writing this chapter. Can you guess where I am?*

Sanremo, Italy is where I am. Unless you're a mathematical genius (or a geography teacher), I think most of us will have a hard time mapping a latitude and longitude to an actual place.

This is why we have geocoding, which will take an address and give the corresponding lat/lon[10] for it. Decoding is mostly called "reverse geocoding" but I find it very confusing and prefer to think I'm decoding a geographical coordinate. It will then translate that coordinate in the picture to the actual location, which, as you can see in Figure 3-5, Photos.app does wonderfully on the Mac.

---

[10]This is short for latitude and longitude and is commonly used to spare the repetive spelling. You can also use (like shown in the picture) lat/long.

Figure 3-5. *Photos.app on the Mac shows the exact location — near the sea — where this picture was taken*

Now if you have paid attention to what I was saying, the pin shown on the map isn't a reverse geocoding. The name *Bussana, Liguria, Italy*, though, is. We won't get into the details of why it doesn't say Sanremo, but I can assure you that I'm in the Liguria region, which really is around 43.81/7.77.

If you enter Sanremo, Italy on a website for finding lat/lon[11] you'll have **43.819825** and **7.774883** as an answer. This is where the accuracy plays a role. You won't always be able to have that accuracy even if I would have entered a specific street and number. It all depends on which hardware was used when getting that location.

---

[11]E.g., `https://latlong.net` is a simple and useful website for that.

Show Me the Code

Let's start with the simpler, reverse geocoding. Say you have a CLLocation (with the previous coordinates) for which you'd want to know the actual address. The code in Listing 3-3 will display the output in Listing 3-4.

The important object here is the CLGeocoder, which can be used for both direction of geocoding.

Listing 3-3. This Is How You'd Simply Print the Found Placemarks

```
let coder = CLGeocoder()
let location = CLLocation(latitude: 43.819825,
                          longitude: 7.774883)
coder.reverseGeocodeLocation(location) { (pms, error) in
    print(error ?? "no error")
    print(pms   ?? "no placemarks")
}
```

Listing 3-4. This Is the Output the Previous Code Would Give

```
no error
[Giardini Regina Elena, Giardini Regina Elena,
18038 Sanremo, Province of Imperia, Italy @
<+43.81982500,+7.77488300> +/- 100.00m, region CLCircularRegion
(identifier:'<+43.81982499,+7.77488300> radius 141.68',
center:<+43.81982499,+7.77488300>, radius:141.68m)]
```

As you can see, the result is either an error or a list of places. It's important to have a look at the structure of a CLPlacemark. It has the following properties:

- CLLocation

- CLRegion

- NSTimeZone

And then there are the address dictionary properties, where it's really useful to look at Listing 3-5, being extracted from `CLPlacemark.h`.

Listing 3-5. Shows the Type (Mostly Strings, with the Last One Being an Array) of Properties We Have, but Also an Example

```
NSString *name; // eg. Apple Inc.
NSString *thoroughfare; // street name, eg. Infinite Loop
NSString *subThoroughfare; // eg. 1
NSString *locality; // city, eg. Cupertino
NSString *subLocality;
        // neighborhood, common name, eg. Mission District
NSString *administrativeArea; // state, eg. CA
NSString *subAdministrativeArea;
        // county, eg. Santa Clara
NSString *postalCode; // zip code, eg. 95014
NSString *ISOcountryCode; // eg. US
NSString *country; // eg. United States
NSString *inlandWater; // eg. Lake Tahoe
NSString *ocean; // eg. Pacific Ocean
NSArray<NSString *> *areasOfInterest;
        // eg. Golden Gate Park
```

It's important to be familiar with some uncommon names like thoroughfare for the *street* or subThoroughfare for the *number*. I guess the reason for those cryptic namings is that — like anything that has to do with regional settings[12] — not every address has a street.

Think about some countries not using a postal/zip code or streets not having a number. This is a weird dictionary/set of properties because — well — the earth is complicated. See inlandWater and ocean: I don't think we want to give them a street and number.

---

[12]My friend Joachim Kurz gave a talk dealing with regional setting during iOSDevUK 2018. www.youtube.com/watch?v=Y_YZg7qKUfE&t=16425s

Even Without Localization Services Enabled

Okay: the previous dictionary list of properties can only be obtained via a coordinate. It might be your current coordinate (as a user) if you agreed to give your user location, but bear in mind that it might also come from an online database or — as we'll see in a following chapters — from your contacts or calendar database.

Now what if all we have is an address, and we'd like the coordinates. As an example, I'm going to take that address that I just got, but here again it could come from anywhere — even a free text entry.

There are a few convenient methods in CLGeocoder, so let's see one in Listing 3-6. This one shows the usage of postalAddress, which is something we'll develop in the chapter about the Contacts API, but conveniently for our sample it should also be in a CLPlacemark object.

Listing 3-6. The pms Object from Listing 3-3 Is Used Here to Extract the postalAddress, which Will Give Us Basically the Same Object at the End

```
guard let placemark = pms?.first else {
    print("no placemarks")
    return
}
guard let address = placemark.postalAddress else {
    print("This placemark has no postalAddress")
    return
}
coder.geocodePostalAddress(address, completionHandler:
{ (placemarks, error) in
    print(error ?? "no error")
    print(placemarks ?? "no placemarks")
})
```

Note that to be able to use postalAddress you'll need to import the Contacts framework.

The gist of this code is to find that exact same information (well, not the same instance but they should retrieve the same data) that we found in the previous example.

You obviously will always have an info (the actual address or the coordinate) in the output that you already have/gave in the input.

By now, I hope that you can see the privacy concern here. It's not only that by giving your current location as a user it can be physically retrieved (address) and shown on a map (MKAnnotation, see Chapter 2), but it's also that even if you don't, if the developer has access to your address, he will be able to retrieve your location.

Fixed Location or Moving Location

I might have been too dramatic at the end of that last paragraph. There's a huge difference between getting one coordinate and getting access for an app to your current location at any time.

It's one thing to potentially know where I live (which might be a bigger problem in terms of privacy), but it's another to know all the time where I am moving.

The delegate method didUpdateLocations is exactly that. As the user moves around, it will be called, from the moment when the app startUpdatingLocation() was called to when it then stops with startUpdatingLocation().

You can exercise this in the Simulator via the menu *Debug → Location* and then choose, for example, a *City Run*.

Elevation of Privileges

Let's start in Figure 3-6 by seeing what kind of alert the user will see if the developer directly asks `requestAlwaysAuthorization()` until iOS 12. You can learn a lot about the changes that were made in iOS 13 by watching *What's New in Core Location* from WWDC 2019 on Apple's developer portal[13].

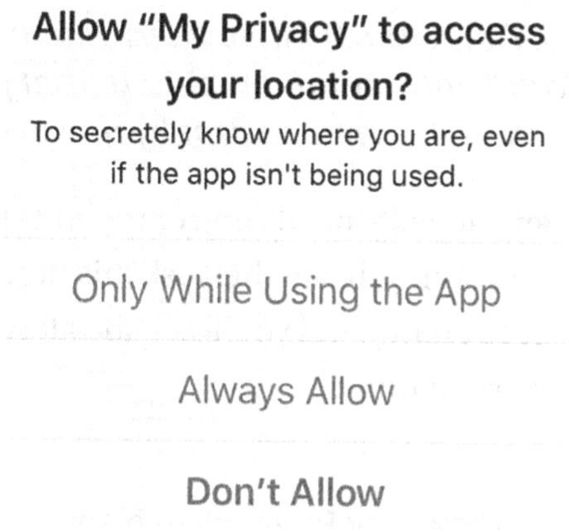

Allow "My Privacy" to access your location?
To secretely know where you are, even if the app isn't being used.

Only While Using the App

Always Allow

Don't Allow

Figure 3-6. *The alert that will be shown if you don't elevate your privileges in iOS 11 or 12. How it looks like in iOS 13 is shown in shown in Figure 3-1.*

The user is more likely to tap on *Don't Allow* than anything else, if you ask me.

Instead, here's how you should do it: the right way. Start by asking `requestWhenInUseAuthorization()`. This will show the alert in Figure 3-7, which is much more likely to be accepted. You see, it's interesting that so many developers think they'll ask for the full Monty although they actually don't need it!

---

[13]https://developer.apple.com/wwdc19/705

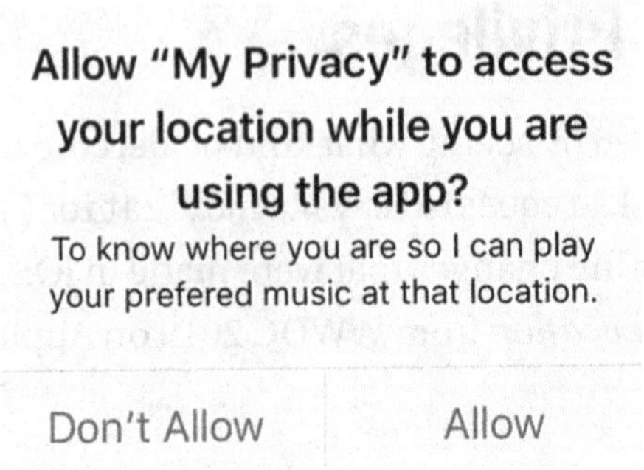

**Allow "My Privacy" to access
your location while you are
using the app?**

To know where you are so I can play
your prefered music at that location.

Don't Allow | Allow

Figure 3-7. *The nice Don't Allow/Allow alert you might remember
from the old days. Valid only for until iOS 12 in that form but the
concept of elevation stays the same, except by any means forced.*

Later, when your app actually needs one of the APIs that
requires background location, you can then ask this time
`requestAlwaysAuthorization()` and you'll see the alert in Figure 3-8,
which has as well only two options.

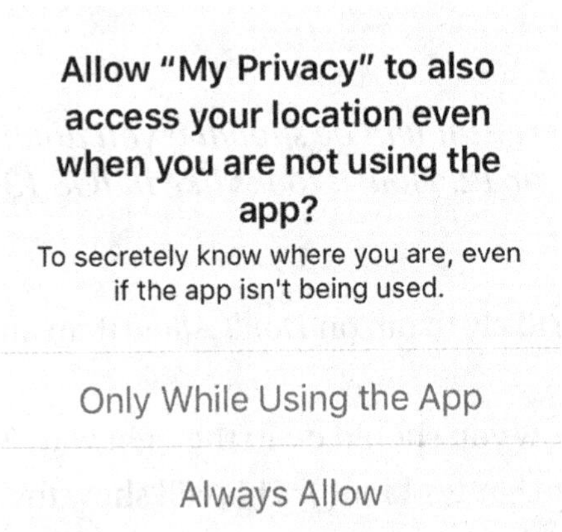

**Allow "My Privacy" to also
access your location even
when you are not using the
app?**

To secretely know where you are, even
if the app isn't being used.

Only While Using the App

Always Allow

Figure 3-8. *That alert is stacked because of the length of the text, but
can you spot something in particular?*

That last *Don't Allow* from Figure 3-6 isn't there anymore! Obviously,
since the user already told you it will be fine to get her location while using
the app, she can't say no anymore. Except the user can — in the settings.

In iOS 13 a similar prompt will appear that lets a user elevate an app's authorization to *Always* or stay *When In Use*.

As we mentioned in the chapter about the common API Elements, never assume you got the authorization just because you already asked.

Less Reasons to Use Always in iOS 13

One of the reason developers had to use the mode *Always* was that some API calls like for example Region Monitoring would require `Always` access and wouldn't be able to deliver events without this authorization, also if those events would be delivered while the App was in use.

This sounds as obscure as it is and the only things that determines if events are delivered now is the combination of the authorization level and the app status. It means if I only have `WhenInUse` I will only get Region Monitoring events delivered when my app is in use.

Remember that until iOS 12 I wouldn't have received those, even though the app was in used.

Temporary Authorization iOS 13

The button that says Allow Once in Figure 3-1 (for iOS 13) is that new feature. It functions in Provisional way as well. Just like you can go from `WhenInUse` to either Always or back to `WhenInUse` with Provisional Always Authorization, this one will allow you to move from the `.notDetermined` state to `.authorizedWhenInUse` and back to `.notDetermined` as soon as your app isn't in use anymore.

This means the next time the app is active, the user will get the prompt again if the app asks again. The obvious advice here from a developer to a developer is to not ask this multiple times but obviously if possible only onces and by any means if possible after a user action.

MapKit Knows Your Country

Even if you don't give an app access to your location services, even if the whole OS doesn't have access to location services, it will most probably get it from your IP Address and center the Maps to your country.

Figure 3-9 shows that although I don't even allow the system to localize me, thus even less an app, it knows that at the time of this writing I'm in this wonderful country in the south of Europe. When I'm at home in Germany, the map is centered toward Germany.

Figure 3-9. The map is centered on my current approximate location, probably based on IP tables

Sure, it's convenient, but from a privacy perspective this is concerning. I think it should be considered that if I don't allow an app (and/or the system) to have the information about where I am, then it also shouldn't look up the geo-ip-databases instead.

Note the Arrow

Figure 3-10 shows the iOS settings with the legend at the bottom describing the role of the arrow. It can be full (two different colors) or hollow and will show you what happened.

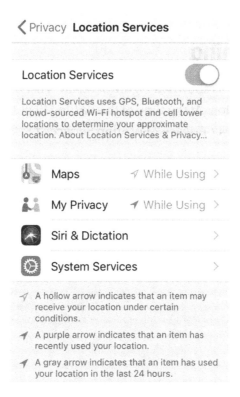

Figure 3-10. *A hint at how the installed apps use your location*

Look what happens in Figure 3-11 when I then started My Privacy again and it asked for my current position.

Figure 3-11. *Here's a variation of the previous figure*

As a user, it would be smart to look at this list of apps now and then and potentially revoke the allowances you gave.

One More Thing

The system services, as shown in Figure 3-12, are a list of things that Apple does with your location. At the time of this writing (iOS 12.4 and iOS 13 Beta 4), it's in Settings / Privacy / Location Services / System Services, at the very bottom.

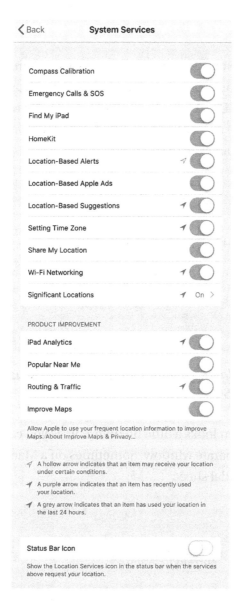

Figure 3-12. *The long list of things that Apple does and you might not know*

On the Mac

There's obviously no concept of *When in Use* (a Mac being very
multitasking) but other than that, as you can see on Figure 3-13, I get a
blue point — my MKUserLocation — where I am while writing this line. To
reach that, I used the exact same code. I'll let the Catalyst (iPad App on a
Mac) part for you as an exercice.

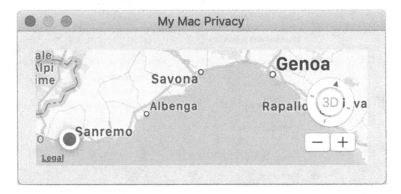

Figure 3-13. *Displaying where I am in a Mac app uses the same
technique as on iOS*

The authorization looks a little bit different, as you can see in
Figure 3-14. It's a separate window. Sometimes on a Mac, a window like
this appears as a modal sheet.

Figure 3-14. *This will be shown to the user of your app whenever
your code makes a request for its current location*

Again, the very good thing about such alerts from the system is that they are from the system. You don't get to decide if you show them or not.

Conclusion

Location is a sensible topic because it tells others where you are, and depending on who is *other* and what their purpose with this information is, it might be a serious breach into your privacy.

Also, it's one of the very few topics in this book that is related directly to hardware: the GPS, the Wi-Fi chip, the GSM chip. It means it's also not only privacy-related but also an energy consumption subject.

CHAPTER 4

Contacts

The Contacts framework, formerly called the AddressBook framework in C, was probably my first real understanding of what can be done wrong (and right) by developers.

Because contacts are an essential part of many apps, whenever speaking about privacy, the most important thing is a single entity of data. Therefore, we'll start this chapter discussing the properties of a contact.

Another aspect of data is the people — or the *amount* of people we select. To illustrate this I'll use a comparison of the good, the bad, and the ugly developer, and I'll end the chapter by showing you how we do it using the out-of-process pickers.

The (Long) List of Properties

The following list gives you an idea of the many things a developer can use whenever users grant access to the database with `CNContactStore().requestAccess(for: .contacts)`. Note that they are all prefixed with `CNContact`.

© Manuel Carrasco Molina 2019
M. Carrasco Molina, *Karma-based API on Apple Platforms*,
https://doi.org/10.1007/978-1-4842-4291-9_4

NamePrefixKey	GivenNameKey
MiddleNameKey	FamilyNameKey
PreviousFamilyNameKey	NameSuffixKey
NicknameKey	OrganizationNameKey
DepartmentNameKey	JobTitleKey
PhoneticGivenNameKey	PhoneticMiddleNameKey
PhoneticFamilyNameKey	PhoneticOrganizationNameKey
BirthdayKey	NonGregorianBirthdayKey
NoteKey	ImageDataKey
ThumbnailImageDataKey	ImageDataAvailableKey
TypeKey	PhoneNumbersKey
EmailAddressesKey	PostalAddressesKey
DatesKey	UrlAddressesKey
RelationsKey	SocialProfilesKey
InstantMessageAddressesKey	

Apple removed support for getting the notes from a Contact in iOS 13. It means that any code using this will crash. I suggest not using this key in your code anymore and release a new version soon or use it conditionally in previous versions of iOS.

As you can see, this is a lot of information that is "let loose." Now it doesn't mean you as a developer should ask for access to each of these properties.

Different Kinds of Developers

Like the classic Clint Eastwood movie, "The Good, the Bad, and the Ugly," there can be three types of developers. Let's quickly look at them now.

The Good Developer

You could simply... You **should** simply (as we show in Listing 4-1) access only a few properties, and this for only one or two persons.

Listing 4-1. How You Can Be a Good Developer (Privacy-Wise, Karma-Wise) and Only Access a Subset of the User's Private Data

```
let predicate =
    CNContact.predicateForContacts(matchingName: "John")
let keys = [CNContactGivenNameKey, CNContactFamilyNameKey]
CNContactStore().unifiedContacts(matching: predicate,
                                 keysToFetch: keys)
```

Here we will only get *John* and *Appleseed*. You had the first already, so I'm not going to finger point at you if you ask for a few more properties, or a few more people, but you get the idea.

The Bad Developer

The bad developer would simply not care about this keysToFetch property and thus retrieve all the properties, as shown in Listing 4-2.

I won't write the code here because it's simply listing all the properties we previously did, in the same way as Listing 4-1, but instead of 2 or 3 it will be 20 or 30 properties. That is a lot of properties, but at least that is only for one or two people.

Listing 4-2. The Pretty Huge Amount of Information a CNContact Holds

```
<CNContact: givenName=John, familyName=Appleseed,
organizationName=(null), phoneNumbers=(
        <CNLabeledValue: label=_$!<Mobile>!$_, value=
        <CNPhoneNumber: stringValue=888-555-5512>,
```

```
        <CNLabeledValue: label=_$!<Home>!$_, value=
        <CNPhoneNumber: stringValue=888-555-1212>
), emailAddresses=(
        <CNLabeledValue: label=_$!<Work>!$_,
                    value=John-Appleseed@mac.com>
), postalAddresses=(
        <CNLabeledValue: label=_$!<Work>!$_,
                        value=
<CNPostalAddress:
        street=3494 Kuhl Avenue, city=Atlanta, postalCode=30303,
        country=USA, countryCode=us>>,

    <CNLabeledValue: label=_$!<Home>!$_, value=
<CNPostalAddress:
                street=1234 Laurel Street, city=Atlanta
                postalCode=30303, country=USA, countryCode=us>>
)>
```

This is not even everything, because if you'd fill for example the previously mentioned CNContactRelationsKey I could totally know as a developer who is your mother, your spouse, and so on. As for everyone saying "I have nothing to hide," ask them if they really are never critical of anyone and what if a bad person got their hands on some of this information.

Note that you'll only get the properties you request **and** those that are filled in the contact; but also note that should you need after that to access a property you didn't retrieve, your app **will crash** unless you retrieve this additional required property.

The Ugly Developer

Listing 4-3 shows you what many apps on the App Store do nowadays. This is a terribly sad situation — and the worst is to come.

Listing 4-3. shows what Angel Eyes as a developer could have done

```
let store = CNContactStore()
let predicate = CNContact.predicateForContactsInContainer(
    withIdentifier: store.defaultContainerIdentifier()
)
```

That takes the whole database, all the properties. Even worse, there's no way to tell as a user what kind of information the developer has taken and no way to protect some of the fields, contacts, or group of contacts.

I regularly write all sorts of reports at `https://feedbackassistant.apple.com`, the replacement for retired Bug Reporter, and duplicate them at `http://openradar.me` so others can see them.[1]

Sadly, Apple's only way of indicating the importance of a bug report someone wrote is with the "Recent Similar Reports" field, let alone having access to the list of bugreports/reviewers. Even when they mark your bug report as a duplicate of another one, all they give you is the number. You can then use this number and see if you can find it on OpenRadar.

You Don't Need to Ask Permission

Remember what Apple says in its App Store Review Guidelines, (iii) Data Minimization.[2]

> *Where possible, use the out-of-process picker or a share sheet rather than requesting full access to protected resources like Photos or Contacts.*

---

[1]You can find my reports on OpenRadar under the username **mc** or **manuel** (changed e-mail at one point), and I regularly post them on Twitter as **stuffmc**.

[2]`https://developer.apple.com/app-store/review/guidelines`

In short, the application asks to open a file, and the out-of-process picker grants the application access to the file the user chooses and returns a document portal path. In our case, the file is a contact and you can use the out-of-process picker or a share sheet to select multiple contacts. At the time of this writing though, note that there's a bug with filtering the selection in multiple mode.[3] Let's start with single selection, in Figure 4-1. When you tap the button that says "1" the list of contacts appear. This is then the out-of-process view controller.

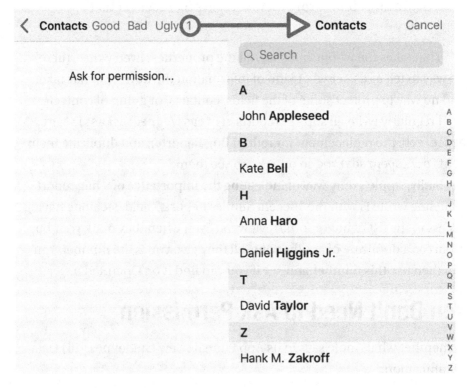

Figure 4-1. *A single selection picker that only allows selecting one contact*

---

[3]http://openradar.me/45621483 — This 3 years old bug since iOS 9 seems like it might stay in iOS 13. To be continued.

Let's see in Listing 4-4 how you can access one or multiple contacts without the need of having access to the entire address book.

It also shows the delegate call-back that is part of your app. The delegation concept is one that also helps protects your privacy by getting (in this case) from the system only the contact that the user selected.

Listing 4-4. This Is How You'd Display a Picker and React When a Contact Is Selected. This Is All Out-of-Process and Thus Requires No Access or Authorization

```
let picker = CNContactPickerViewController()
picker.delegate = self
present(picker, animated: true) {
  // The first time, you might explain
  // the user he needs to select a contact
}

func contactPicker(_ picker: CNContactPickerViewController
        , didSelect contact: CNContact) {
  // Now use contact and its properties.
}
```

Note that this picker, as well as its delegate, are not in the `Contacts` but rather in the `ContactsUI` framework.

Select Multiple Contacts

All you have to do to select multiple contacts is to replace the delegate method for single use with the one for multiple use like we see in Listing 4-5.

Figure 4-2 shows what this looks like. Very similar to the previous one except you don't tap a contact but you check it and then tap *Done*.

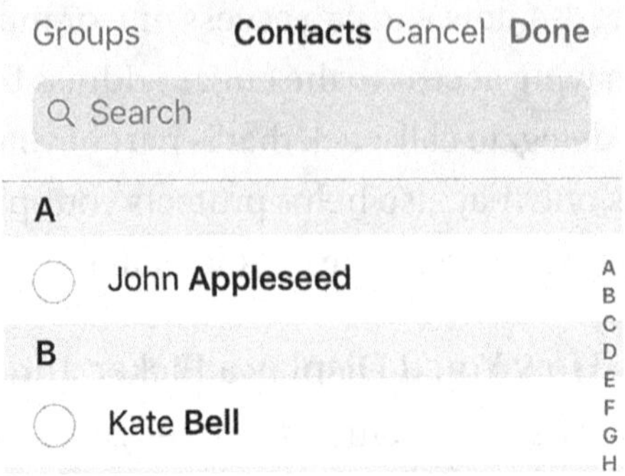

Figure 4-2. *The multiple selection picker*

The only drawback is that since it's based on the delegate method, as soon as you implement the multiple version, the single version will be ignored.

It means that if you have a case where it's sometimes multiple and sometimes single, you'll need 2 delegate objects. It's a bit of a problem but since it's usually a good idea for the clarity of your code to not have the delegate in the same class, it's one we can live with.

Listing 4-5. Implementing the Following Delegate Method Will Make the Previously One Shown Be Ignored

```
func contactPicker(_ picker: CNCPVC
           didSelect contacts: [CNContact]) {
  // Here you'll get an array of contacts.
}
```

What Was That with Location?

Throughout this book you'll see that if a developer can't get information with one door, he will try the next one. Contacts don't really have a geolocation themselves but they do have an address, usually.

The code in Listing 4-6 shows something mentioned also in the chapter about location, but it's useful to have this mentioned in both chapters. You can take a `postalAddress` and geocode it, which will give you coordinates you can place on a map.

Listing 4-6. This Is How I Can Geocode a postalAddress

```
CLGeocoder().geocodePostalAddress(address) { (pms, err) in
    pms?.forEach {
        mapView.addAnnotation($0)
    }
}

extension CLPlacemark: MKAnnotation {
    public var coordinate: CLLocationCoordinate2D {
        get { return location!.coordinate }
    }
}
```

Now I totally see you crying that `location!` is a terrible idea. You are totally right, so we could write a code like in Listing 4-7 but that isn't much better. Instead, the caller of coordinate or the adder on the `mapView` should check that the placemark has a non-nil location.

This way you either replace the (0,0) coordinate with an error throwing, or you (developer) live with the risk of force-unwrapping, which should never crash if you previously tested correctly!

Listing 4-7. What We Could Do to Avoid Force Unwrapping. Not So Much Better

```
guard let location = self.location else {
  return CLLocationCoordinate2D(latitude: 0, longitude: 0)
}
return location.coordinate
```

Managed Contacts

Mobile Device Management (MDM) is a server-side set of rules that manages how a device is used, usually in an Enterprise environment. The MAM part (Mobile Application Manager) decides for example which Managed Apps are installed on a device.

In the same way, a mail server like Microsoft Exchange can be configured for its contacts to be qualified as Managed Contacts. The same way as there is an "Open In" rule that doesn't allow data to be lost from an Enterprise App to a non-Enterprise app, there is, finally since a release just before iOS 12, a mini revolution for privacy.

This shows to a consumer app (let's take a Messenger app you use to talk to your family as an example) only those contacts who are private. This way, your business contacts will never land on some random server.

The beauty of this is that it's totally transparent for the API — and there's nothing the user can do, except being itself a Managed App, to circumvent this.

On the Mac

Hey! Good news again! It's literally the same code on the Mac. As you can see on Figure 4-3, the authorization window (which uses the string I added in `Info.plist`) shows whenever my app asks for full access to the contacts database.

Figure 4-3. *The alert that the system displays, which is luckily not in the control of the developer*

Here again I did some experimenting by displaying the amount of contacts in the console (basically the code in Listings 4-1 and 4-3) and the second button displays the persons having my last name, which ended up being some people where I was born and raised and others where I live and raise my kids.

You can see the result in Figure 4-4, which is from the Demo/Sample Mac app *My Mac Privacy* that goes with this book.

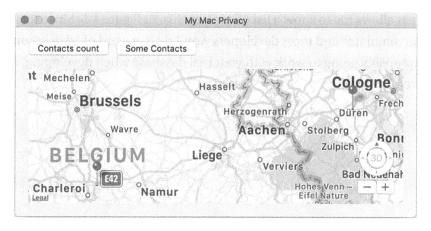

Figure 4-4. *The map with two members of my family: one in the town in which I was born in Belgium, one where I usually live in Germany*

The Picker on the Mac

It's a little bit different than on iOS but not so much, as you can see in Listing 4-8. Basically CNContactPicker is an NSObject instead of being a View Controller, so you don't present it but instead use a method that does it as a popup.

Listing 4-8. The Mac Version of the Contact Picker and Its Delegate Method

```
let picker = CNContactPicker()
picker.delegate = self
picker.showRelative(to: NSZeroRect,
                    of: view, preferredEdge: .maxX)

func contactPicker(_ picker: CNContactPicker,
        didSelect contact: CNContact) {
    print(contact)
}
```

That allows me to show a list of contacts like in Figure 4-5. Since there's no Mac simulator and most developers won't do it, a word of advice: you're most probably going to work with your real database when developing, so be careful.

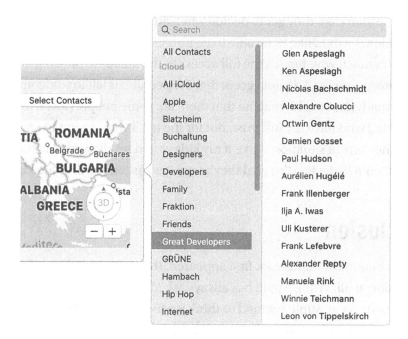

Figure 4-5. *When I tap the button "Select Contacts," I display a list of contacts from which I can pick*

This not only for the data (after all, this is a book about privacy) but for the *amount* of data. I have over 2,000 contacts. It's way too much and I need to sort, but I'm pretty sure it's pretty common to have built such a list after many years.

By the way, this works for photos as well. If you work with your library, be ready — mine is over 120,000 photos!

Who's Contact? My Contact!

Here is a proposition I'm making to Apple: the idea of the ownership of my data. There are countless websites where I'm myself responsible for maintaining my contact data, yet on iOS it's my friend who decides which phone number is the current one I have.

Worse than that, they get to decide when an app accesses **my** contact information. I would like to be able to be notified when an app is going to read my contact, whether it's the full access to the database or using an out-of-process picker. I do not accept that the decision is left to someone else.

Alternatively, I could imagine that there are some people (loved one, family, etc.) who have my full trust, but for the rest I would want to know. To me, the current situation is like if my kids would be allowed to install any app on their iOS device. I'm glad they're not, yet, as long as they are kids.

Conclusion

When the contacts framework first appeared, there was no asking of permission at all. While Apple has always asked you to have your location, some engineers at Apple seemed to think it was okay to steal your whole list of friends, family, and professional contacts.

It's gotten better — way better — and we have the out-of-process pickers nowadays, but there's still so many fine-grained options that I'd like to see arise.

CHAPTER 5

Calendar and Events

The Calendar Framework is called EventKit, and its corresponding user interfaces are in EventKitUI. The basic underlying model allows you to describe a calendar as well as a single event.

The hierarchy is that the central database has a set of calendars, while each calendar has the events representing the actual entry (e.g., every Monday at 10 AM).

Events, just like Contacts, can be augmented with geolocation information; or if they only have an address, this can be used to geocode it.

This chapter digs deep into this, as well as taking note of the special case about the birthday calendar. It wraps up by showing the set of user interfaces that the system has built in that will make your task easier.

The Models

At the heart of every query that will be made is the Calendar Entity. We have the models; in fact, it's the same as for Contact. But since many things/ideas are common, I'm purposely not always being repetitive.

As you can see in Listing 5-1, there's not much interesting in there, or at least that's what one could believe.

© Manuel Carrasco Molina 2019
M. Carrasco Molina, *Karma-based API on Apple Platforms*,
https://doi.org/10.1007/978-1-4842-4291-9_5

Listing 5-1. A Single Calendar. Standard on iOS Is, e.g., Home & Work

```
EKCalendar {
      title = Calendar;
      type = Local;
      allowsModify = YES;
      color = #FF1493;
}
```

Sadly, the API still doesn't allow the user to decide to give access to some calendars and not others. Also, like the Contact API, it doesn't provide a way to access only some groups.

Listing 5-2 shows that there are different types and you can choose one, but there's no real option for the user to give specific permission to one calendar and not another one.

Listing 5-2. The Different Types (Sources Actually) of Calendar

```
public enum EKCalendarType : Int {
      case local
      case calDAV
      case exchange
      case subscription
      case birthday
}
```

The calendar type birthday is very interesting from a privacy perspective because it'll contain a list of contacts for which you have entered a birthday.

Calendar Chooser

You might have found `EKCalendarChooser` but this is — to me — just a joke. Sure, it allows a user to select a calendar and the developer can do as shown in Listing 5-3, but there's no hint that this is done.

Listing 5-3. The Usage of a Calendar Chooser

```
let store = EKEventStore()
let cal = EKCalendarChooser(selectionStyle: .single,
                           displayStyle: .allCalendars,
                           entityType: .event,
                           eventStore: store)
cal.delegate = self
navigationController?.pushViewController(cal, animated: true)

func calendarChooserSelectionDidChange(
                _ calendarChooser: EKCalendarChooser)
{
    let cals = calendarChooser.selectedCalendars
    let pred = store.predicateForEvents(withStart: from, end:
            to, calendars: cals)
    // You could use that predicate...
}
```

That last line of code says *could*. It means that even though the developer might ask you, for example, which calendar you'd want to use (e.g., to display the list of events), it could still grab any of the others (or all) of the calendars in the back of the user which couldn't know.

What Have You Done?

The power of the calendar API is basically to know what you have done in the past. Luckily — and it really isn't for privacy reasons[1] — if you wanted to know what I've done since my birth, you'd need more than one query; but hey, performance won't be a problem with today's hardware.

So there's sadly nothing that prevents us from doing — in practice — the query in Listing 5-4. In actual practice this will return only what I've done while Jesus wasn't at Kindergarten yet, but all it takes is an easy loop. So, if you see 0 events returned in this case, always remember your result might not be the one you think.

Listing 5-4. The Maximum Span Will Always Be 4 Years

```
store.predicateForEvents(withStart: Date.distantPast,
                                end: Date.distantFuture,
                         calendars: calendar)
```

Keep in mind that Date.distantPast is 0000-12-30 00:00:00 +0000 (Year 0…), while Date.distantFuture is 4001-01-01 00:00:00 +0000, which should be good until the release of iOS 1993. Yes, that is a version number.

For this Book I first did a very rough computation of 4 years, like in Listing 5-5, but if you ever need to compute this you really should look at the dateByAdding methods in Calendar, which I did in Listing 5-6. It's not only nicer, but it accounts for the years where we have 366 days. (And did you know our years weren't always 365 days and our months 28/29/30/31

---

[1]For performance reasons, this method matches only those events within a 4-year time span. If the date range between startDate and endDate is greater than 4 years, it is shortened to the first 4 years. — Thanks @michel_fortin on coreint.slack.com for the hint. https://developer.apple.com/documentation/eventkit/ekeventstore/1507479-predicateforevents

days?) Never underestimate Date and Time[2] algorithms or, for example, right to left languages. Those things aren't trivial at all and you should always rely on the API that Apple already provided for you.

Listing 5-5. A First Attempt at Computing 4 Years Ago. Pretty Wrong

```
let years = Date(timeIntervalSinceNow: -60*60*24*365*4)
let pred = store.predicateForEvents(withStart: years,
                                    end: Date(),
                                calendars: local)

store.events(matching: predicate).forEach {
    // Now $0 is a single EKEvent
    print($0.title)
}
```

Listing 5-6. A Better Approach to Compute 4 Years

```
var components = DateComponents()
components.year = -4
let years = NSCalendar.current.date(byAdding: components,
                                    to: Date())
```

Geolocating Your Appointments

As mentioned in the chapter about Locations, many system apps — when they first run — ask if it's okay to use your location. In the case of the

---

[2]Watch "Solutions to Common Date and Time Challenges", a session from WWDC 2013 at https://developer.apple.com/wwdc13/227. It might be over 6 years old, but it's still very much relevant — and now to iOS as well.

Calendar app (or really any app that would save an event in your location database[3]), this might be used like in Listing 5-7 to retrieve your location.

Listing 5-7. Each Event Might Directly Have a Latitude and Longitude

```
store.events(matching: predicate).forEach {
    if $0.structuredLocation?.geoLocation != nil {
        // do something with that CLLocation
    }
}
```

That being said, even if you didn't give access to your current location (and really, most events you enter in your calendar aren't at the current location anyway), the Calendar app will offer you a list of places and will then directly add the latitude and longitude. Even if it didn't do it, Listing 5-8 shows you how the beautiful — yet not privacy-friendly — APIs from Apple allow you to geocode an address.

Listing 5-8. Need to Geocode An Address String?

```
if let location = event.location {
    CLGeocoder().geocodeAddressString(location) {
    (placemarks, error) in
        if let location = placemarks?.first?.location       {
        self.annotate(location: location)
        }
    }
}
```

---

[3]The difference here being that such an app would also need access to your calendar, which the calendar doesn't ask. The Camera doesn't ask for access to your camera either!

What Exactly Is in the Structured Location?

It is also important to know what kinds of information are stored there (and this is what is shown in Listing 5-9). You can tell, for example, that a geolocation (which is a standard CLLocation) is always a bit more than just a latitude and longitude. It also has information about the speed, the course, and many things that could, for example, tell someone if I was just walking, not moving, or in a rapid train.[4]

Listing 5-9. The EKStructuredLocation Has Some Interesting Information

```
{
    title   = Lima;
    address = ;
    geo     = <-12.05929000,-77.03006000>
              +/- 0.00m (speed -1.00 mps / course -1.00)
              @ 5/27/18,
              5:26:17 PM Central European Summer Time;

    abID    = (null);
    routing = (null);
    radius  = 9178.047384;
}
```

So even if I didn't use the geolocation of images, I would be able to show you the images here by simply matching the date and time of the images with the date and time of the event. The general idea here is that if we don't get the information from one side or one API, we might be able to get it from the other side.

---

[4]This is in fact what Felix Krause does to detect.location at https://krausefx.com/privacy. He finds the fastest photos, but can also tell if a user has attended college. Frightening, isn't it?! Felix is a great inspiration for the community of people interested in the ethics behind Privacy.

I'll Show You Where You Were

Most of the demo app turns around location, because it's a central part of privacy, and probably the oldest concern in iOS land.

This is what I'm demoing in Figure 5-1, where I display in a map where you were (and when), without having access to your current location.

Figure 5-1. *Displaying the locations I found in your calendar is easy*

That is, I and my app don't have access but the Calendar app does, and we ricochet to your location this way.

Again and again, the hardest thing for Apple to decide here is what is fine-grained enough to respect your privacy and not too much, to make apps still usable.

Once I have access to an event, as described in Listing 5-10, there is also much other information that we can show.

I could also open the URL attached to the event, e-mail all your friends who are invited to this event, and so on and so on...

Listing 5-10. This is What an Event Looks Like

```
EKEvent <0x608000110bc0>
{
        title               = Hanging Around;
        location            = Lima;
        calendar            = EKCalendar;
        alarms              = (null);
        URL                 = http://apple.com;
        lastModified        = 2018-05-27 14:06:12;
        startTimeZone       = America/Lima;
        location            = Lima;
        structuredLocation  = EKStructuredLocation <...>;
        startDate           = 2018-05-23;
        endDate             = 2018-05-23 15:00:00;
        allDay              = 0;
        floating            = 0;
        recurrence          = (null);
        attendees           = (null);
        travelTime          = (null);
        startLocation       = (null);
};
```

As you can tell, I have a few convenient properties like attendees that would give me a list of contacts (name and e-mail address) without having access to your Contacts database.

I could also learn a lot about your habits by analyzing the recurrence property. For this book, I do have to play the bad guy. It's obviously a risk that a (hopefully small) amount of people use this book for bad purposes, but it's a necessary step in evangelizing for Apple platforms to be the best in terms of user privacy.

The Special Birthday Calendar

The problem with this calendar type is that it will display events like we see in Listing 5-11.

If you look closely you can probably find a pattern in the title, which allows us to retrieve a name although we don't have access to the Contacts database.

This is a serious enough breach of your privacy to decide not to save the birthdate of your friends, which is sad, since this is a very convenient way of being reminded and I prefer to have this information in the hands of Apple rather than a social network.

Listing 5-11. Remove the Title's Suffix and You Have a Name

```
EKEvent <0x600002d254d0>
{
        title      = Kate Bell's Birthday;
        startDate  = 2018-01-19 23:00:00 +0000;
        endDate    = 2018-01-20 22:59:59 +0000;
        allDay     = 1;
        recurrence = sRRULE FREQ=YEARLY;INTERVAL=1;
}
```

We are omitting some of the properties but you can see that if we remove `s *Birthday*, we have the name of one of our contacts, as well as her birthday, without the user giving access to the Contacts database.

EventKitUI Still Needs Access

Like the Contacts framework, there's a corresponding set of view controllers that can be used.

The weird part of the `EventKitUI` framework, though, is that it is not out-of-process and it thus needs access to your calendar to display anything.

This heavily defies the purpose of such a UI framework, since in my opinion a big chunk of the benefits of `ContactsUI` resides in the fact that it allows a user to select a contact without giving the developer of this app full access.

Transfer that knowledge to events and I would expect that a user could allow an app access to a single event — or, for example, a day — but if your app doesn't have full access to your calendar you're left with that terrible message in Figure 5-2.

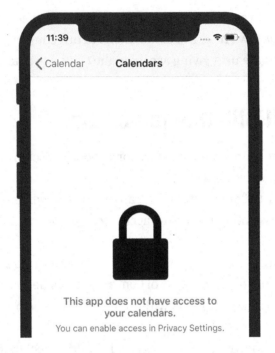

Figure 5-2. *One of the in-app-process pickers*

What's even sadder is that — as mentioned in the introduction of this chapter — you can tell as a developer how old the framework is because there's no link to open the Privacy Settings.

I'm not sure you can expect all users to understand where Privacy Settings are — let alone where the Settings app is.

It's another discussion, but I think the fact that the Settings app *is an app* is a problem. You should be able to go to the settings with some shortcut, or at least the app shouldn't be allowed to be placed in a folder, for example.

I've known some users to move their Settings app into a "Useless" Folder because — believe it or not — some people never ever go into Settings.

At least for highly privacy-related matters like Events and Reminders you'd hope that Apple makes a small update and allows a direct link.

The List of Calendars

We already displayed the code in Listing 5-3 of what we now announce to you as part of the not so amazing EventKitUI. This is the EKCalendarChooser, which has to be either pushed on a view controller or if presented, you should add it to a navigation controller so you have the bottom buttons.

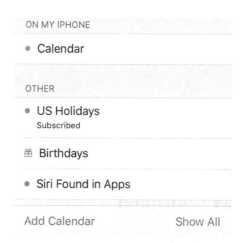

Figure 5-3. *The EKCalendarChoose that can display the list of calendars*

The button Add Calendar surely is neat but, since your app can actually also do it (remember you can't show EKCalendarChooser if you don't have full access!), it's a gimmick we'd rather swap for real privacy.

I'll show you what it does though, in Figure 5-4.

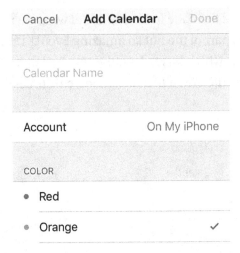

Figure 5-4. The user can add a calendar while staying in your app

The Event View Controller

There's one thing that is useful for editing a single event: it's
EKEventViewController. I decided that in the sample app I would show
it when the "i" button is tapped. I show how it can look (only the data will
change on your side, obviously) in Figure 5-5.

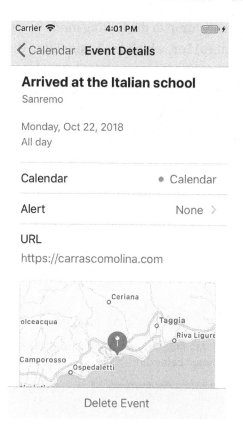

Figure 5-5. *How the Event View Controller looks*

The code in Listing 5-12 is what it takes to display it. The optional allowsEditing is a way to have an **Edit** button at the top right, which does what it says.

Listing 5-12. This Is What It Takes to Use This Other Controller from EventKitUI

```
let eventVC = EKEventViewController()
eventVC.event = events?.first
eventVC.allowsEditing = true
navController?.pushViewController(eventVC, animated: true)
```

You can also directly jump to the Editing mode by using EKEventEditViewController, which works similar to the read-only version.

From a privacy perspective it should be clear to users that the app has access to their calendars. I'm not sure though that it is always clear that the app can read anything — and not only what it shows.

On the Mac

You can do the same with the Event framework that you do on iOS, with the obvious difference that the request looks a bit different, as shown in Figure 5-6, but it uses the same mechanism with the Info.plist as on iOS.

Figure 5-6. The Mac permission request for calendar access

There's no EventKitUI to display an event, so you're left on your own for this.

There's really nothing more to say about the Mac side of things, except I deeply miss this UI part, but if it come we should all hope that it will be out-of-process.

Conclusion

You are now knowledgeable about the API working with Calendars and Events. You can do a lot with them: like, for example, a totally revamped calendar app better than the system one (some have done it) or integrate it into your app.

You could, for example, set up a reminder tomorrow to pick up some food, if you have a food app. However, do not confuse the Calendar API with a local or remote notification, which can be helpful to use as a reminder.

Speaking of reminders, the Reminder apps on iOS and macOS use the same set of APIs, because after all, a reminder is just a calendar entry. All you have to do to apply what you've learned is to use the entity type `.reminder`. It's that easy.

CHAPTER 6

Health and Fitness

Especially if you wear an Apple watch, Apple knows potentially a lot about you. It's important to know how you can use it as a developer if your use case justifies it.

The same as you have the Contacts app or the Calendar app for the corresponding API we already developed in this book, the Health app is where you can see if your code worked.

This chapter essentially discusses two topics: health, as in medical health; and fitness, sport, workouts, which obviously have something to do with health like, for example, heart rate.

Apple talks a lot about privacy — and does a lot for it as well. When there's a talk about HealthKit they **always** have a part about privacy. They don't just speak for 30 seconds about it, but always remember how authorizations and the users' trust are linked to each other.

Adding the Framework

By going into your iOS Target, in the Capabilities tab, and turning that switch on, Xcode will add an `.entitlements` file in your project if you have none. Xcode 11 changes this a bit in that the tab is called "Signing & Capabilities" and instead of a list of checkboxes you use the + button to add a capability.

This XML file contains a set of `<key>` items that either have a `<true/>/<false/>` or, in this case, for example, an empty `<array />`. We'll see later that this might not stay empty, if your app will work with Health Records.

© Manuel Carrasco Molina 2019
M. Carrasco Molina, *Karma-based API on Apple Platforms*,
https://doi.org/10.1007/978-1-4842-4291-9_6

Xcode will also add the `HealthKit.framework`, without which you won't be able to `import HealthKit` into your `.swift` files.

Note that if you ever change the location of this file, you'll probably have to update the Build Setting CODE_SIGN_ENTITLEMENTS, which is a relative path to this file — relative to your .xcodeproj file.

Explain to the User

As a reminder, although this is explained in Chapter 1, you'll need here as well to specify a string for your `.plist`.

Listing 6-1 shows the indication from HealthKit that this is needed. As you can see, it's very descriptive about what kind of properties we want access to, although the string itself is the same for all types.

Listing 6-1. The Log Shown in the Console if I Forget the Important String

```
2018-11-27 12:37:48.681296+0100 My Privacy[26896:8395709]
*** Terminating app due to uncaught exception
'NSInvalidArgumentException', reason:
'NSHealthShareUsageDescription must be set in the app's
Info.plist in order to request read authorization for the
following types: HKCharacteristicTypeIdentifierDateOfBirth,
HKQuantityTypeIdentifierHeight'
```

Central Database

Before HealthKit was introduced in 2014, there already were a lot of health-related apps.

They couldn't really communicate with each other, though. Imagine a Contact app or a Calendar app (also from third-party developers) that couldn't access a central database. That wouldn't be great.

The Core: Quantity & Unit

The simplest piece of information that should stay private is a quantity per unit.

A Unit is used to described, for example, grams, or pounds, or meters, or inches, …

The Source: Object Type

HKObjectType includes things like heart rate, blood pressure, different kind of vitamins, etc. There are over 60 kinds, each one represent something personal from the user, which is why it's important they see it from a privacy perspective.

The Stored Object

Every combination of a quantity and a type — so, an instance — is stored as an HKObject. A child class from it, HKSample, combines:

- Sample type
- Start Date
- End Date

All Properties Are Read-Only!

Yes, you read it right — because it doesn't make a lot of sense to change the data that was recorded yesterday.

It's also a good decision to have immutable properties so nothing can be changed by a mean app.

That being said, you can observe when a property changes, for example, when the user became taller. For that, you can use `HKObserverQuery`. Speaking of which, at the core of some code, we'll show there's going to be an `HKQuery`.

Not Even in Your App's Privacy Settings

I'm not sure if it's for a privacy reason, but tapping on the My Privacy Settings row in the sample app that goes with this book won't show you an entry for Health, although there's a Health section in the Privacy section of the Settings, and the app will be shown there.

Getting the Permission

Before doing anything check `isHealthDataAvailable`, because your code might be running on an iPad, which doesn't support HealthKit.

You only get the chance to show the UI once, but you can always ask for authorization with the method and enum in Listing 6-2.

Also, the reason the enum doesn't contain any hint for read authorizations is a privacy concern.

> *This is because for some data, knowing that the user has blocked access to an app can be just [as] private as knowing the data itself.*

> "Introducing HealthKit"[1], WWDC 2014

---

[1]https://developer.apple.com/wwdc14/203

Think of an app asking the user to read its blood sugar. If they refuse, it might indicate that they are diabetic.

Listing 6-2. The Method and the Enum, Which Aren't Giving Any Info About Read Authorizations

```
if store.authorizationStatus(for: objectType) {
    ...
}

enum HKAuthorizationStatus : Int {
    case notDetermined
    case sharingDenied
    case sharingAuthorized
}
```

Your Missing "me" Card from Contacts

HealthKit has methods to give you, for example, your birthday. As we will soon see in a sample code, HKHealthStore has an instance method: dateOfBirthComponents.

HealthKit even has information that you wouldn't put in your Contacts app, like: *how tall are you* or *what is your weight?*

For some use cases, for example, ordering a T-shirt, it could even be useful to have this information for your friends. Let's see how long it takes for Apple to produce an app similar to Find my Friends or Find my Phone... Find their Weight? Speaking of which, those 2 apps are now one single app called "Find My" in iOS 13, with 2 tabs: People and Devices.

A Different Kind of Alert

You may be used to seeing simple alerts like the access to the Camera, where the only choice is Yes or No. HealthKit does it differently.

101

This alert is displayed when I use the requestAuthorization method, as I do in Listing 6-3 where I'm simply asking permission to read those two parameters. Hence, the screen at Figure 6-1 appears — mind you, with a nice transition.

Listing 6-3. Asking for Access to Date of Birth and Height of the User

```
guard let dateOfBirth = HKObjectType.characteristicType(
                        forIdentifier: .dateOfBirth),

     let height      = HKObjectType.quantityType(
                        forIdentifier: .height) else {
  return
}
store.requestAuthorization(toShare: nil, read:
            [dateOfBirth, height]) { (success, error) in
  if (success) {
    // We'll see later...
  }
}
```

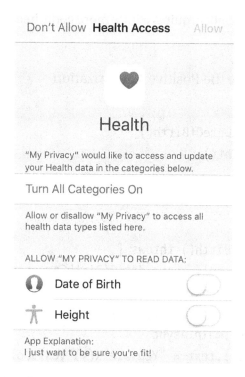

Figure 6-1. *The authorization panel shown by the app the first time*

Keep in mind that the user might change the authorization they gave, at a later time.

If you have nil or zero samples for a given data, like date of birth or height, it could be that the user didn't give access to it, or didn't add the data. There's no way to know, for privacy reasons, but you can of course ask your users to change it, manually.

Now let's get a little deeper with the code in Listing 6-4. This one defines two methods, one for the birthdate, which can throw an exception; and one for how tall (or not) the user is.

The birthdate call on the store can produce an error, can even throw a nilError, and can return a nil value.

103

Gathering the height requires a little more code, because it involves a query.

Listing 6-4. Inside the Positive Authorization

```
do {
  try self.updateDateOfBirth()
  self.updateHeight()
} catch² {
  print(error)
}

func updateDateOfBirth() throws {
  if let bd = try self.store.dateOfBirthComponents().date,
    let y = NSCalendar.current.dateComponents([.year],
              from: bd, to: Date()).year {
    DispatchQueue.main.async {
      self.bdLabel.text = "You are \(y) years old"
    } }
}

func updateHeight() {
  guard let height = height else { return }
  let query = HKSampleQuery(sampleType: height)
                            { (query, samples, eror) in
    DispatchQueue.main.async {
      if let sample = samples?.first as? HKQuantitySample {
        self.hLabel.text = "You are \(sample.quantity)"
      }
    }
}
```

---

[2]**Wondering** where this error variable is coming from? You don't declare it, but it's implicitly declared by Swift. You can change the name or catch a more specific Error but this is out of scope for now.

```
self.store.execute(query)
}
```

You might be wondering where the simple initialization method for HKSampleQuery, which only takes two parameters, comes from. It's an extension I defined, to make my life easier when all I want is the latest value. It's in the sample app; you can find the code there. Also, I was obviously inspired by Apple's sample app "Fit."[3]

Proportional Collection

Coining a term is hard sometimes. Apple got it absolutely right with this one. They not only emphasize that it's important to build trust with the user, but they remind developers constantly — and so will I, obviously — that you shouldn't collect more data than you need.[4]

Remember you can always escalate the permissions. You can start by asking for some permissions and at a later time add more.

It means Apple wants to draw your attention to three things about privacy, namely that you have to ask for:

- **Only what you need**

- **Only when you need it**

- **Every time you need it**

"New Ways to Work with Workouts"

Niharika Bedekar, Fitness Software Engineer.

---

[3]https://developer.apple.com/library/ios/fit_sample
[4]https://developer.apple.com/videos/play/wwdc2018/707/?time=177 •
https://developer.apple.com/videos/play/wwdc2019/708/?time=84

We'll discuss more on this in a very special way when we develop the delicate subject of Health Records later.

It means that if my app starts by asking only the information in Figure 6-1 but I then decide (once the user used a UI to start a Workout) that I not only want to read that information but I also need to write others, I could replace the `toShare: nil` from Listing 6-3 with `toShare: [.workoutType(), distanceType]` and I'll have the screen shown in Figure 6-2 appear.

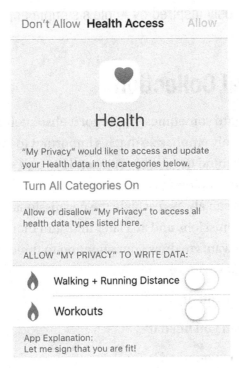

Figure 6-2. *The birthday and height won't be asked again, just the new authorizations*

Note that if your user kills the app — or if you restart your code in Xcode — before taking the decision to accept or refuse authorization, they will appear again.

A User Can Always Change His Mind in the Settings

It's worth saying it again and again. You should always ask for authorization even if your user previously accepted (or rejected) an authorization. In the case of HealthKit, though, it's a bit trickier since you won't know if a read-only authorization was rejected.

Workouts — and Their Maps

There are various aspects of the HealthKit API. The sport one is probably the most used, especially in combination with the Apple Watch.

Although the class `HKWorkoutSession` is only available on Apple Watch,[5] `HKWorkoutRoute` and its corresponding `HKWorkoutRouteBuilder` are luckily available on both. Don't be confused like I was by the generated Headers in Swift.[6]

The reason for my confusion came from the fact that the *My Privacy* sample app has — like Apple recommends in its 2017 WWDC Session *What's new in Health* — a common `HealthManager` helper class.

You should know the difference between looking for the `HKWorkoutRoute.h` file and clicking on the `HKWorkoutRoute` class in your code. The latter will generate an interface specifically for the platform it thinks this class belongs to. It's confusing but, long story short, not being afraid of Objective-C is still an advantage as a developer for Apple Technologies.

Sadly, this session from 2017 hasn't updated the sample code, so you can only follow the slides and watchOS development was still a major pain in 2019, if you ask me. I haven't worked much with watchOS 6 so there's

---

[5]For whatever reason, maybe simply a commercial one.

[6]`https://twitter.com/StuFFmc/status/1074016881420484608`

hope that many things are better — for one thing, independent Watch Apps and thus independent Simulator might be great! There's a wonderful set of APIs, but the tools for debugging are terrible, would be my quote until WWDC 2019. I might revise my opinion hopefully by the end of 2019.

Note that when I started writing this chapter it was still smarter to develop your watchOS extension in Objective-C instead of Swift 4.2 because, since the Swift libraries weren't yet ship with the OS, they needed to be deployed (and that is probably over Bluetooth) from the Watch app (Extension) on the Phone to the Watch. Since we now have Swift 5, a stabilized ABI and many new things with Xcode 11 and watchOS 6, things might be nicer in the near future[7]

Listing 6-5 will suppose that you use Core Location to get the location data, but you sure could use historical data and even create a CLLocation without CLLocationManager.

This code saves geographical information in the HealthKit database, which is in turn displayed in the Health app as shown in Figure 6-3.

More later on that device parameter used to create the route...

Listing 6-5. The Steps to Create a Workout Route

```
// Step 1: Create the route and start CoreLocation
let builder = HKWorkoutRouteBuilder(healthStore: store,
                                    device: nil)

// Step 2: Add locations as the workout is ongoing
func locationManager(_ manager: CLLocationManager,
   didUpdateLocations locations: [CLLocation]) {
```

---

[7]Reminds me of Daniel Steinberg's talk at SwiftConf 2018 — https://youtube.com/watch?v=GzP2oaZRi7Q

```
builder.insertRouteData(locations) { (success, error) in
  // Deal with success & errors...
}
}

// Step 3: After the workout is saved, save the route data
builder.finishRoute(with: workout, metadata: nil) {
                              (workoutRoute, error) in
  // Handle errors...
}
```

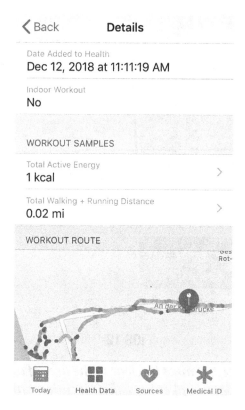

Figure 6-3. *The finished route displayed in the Health app, Workout section*

iOS 12

Figure 6-4. *In iOS 12: It must be clear to the user of a Workout app that both Apple and the app maker have their location data, which they can find in "Show All Data"; In iOS 13: The Health App changed quite a lot on iOS 13 — this is the way to reach your Workout Data.*

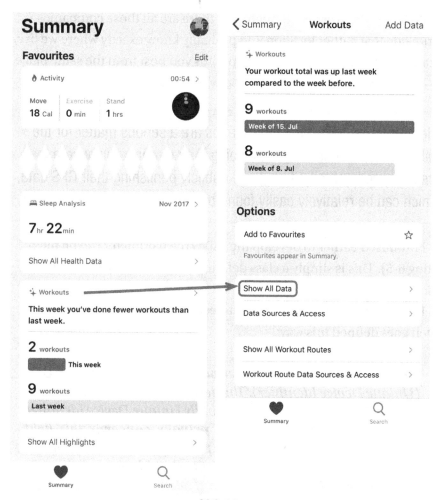

iOS 13

Figure 6-4. *(continued)*

I'm a little bit worried, though, that there are all those companies worldwide that gather location and probably know exactly where we live, because it's trivial to see how many photos you post from the same place or — in this case — the neighborhood where you always run.

Did you know that some fitness apps are a serious matter for the military? Some of those people doing their morning run, where they are supposed not to be found, are publicly publishing their GPS data, which can be relatively easily found by enemies…

I promised earlier to develop the HKDevice parameter (being nil in Listing 6-5). This is simply a class defining a device with a set of strings describing it.

Probably the most cryptic but interesting is udiDeviceIdentifier, which goes defined this way:

> *Represents the device identifier portion of a device's FDA UDI (Unique Device Identifier). The device identifier can be used to reference the FDA's GUDID (Globally Unique Device Identifier Database). Note that **for user privacy concerns** this field should not be used to persist the production identifier portion of the device UDI. HealthKit clients should manage the production identifier independently, if needed.*[8]

Apple Documentation (HKDevice.h)

Figure 6-5 is another example of information found in Details like we showed already in Figure 6-3, except this is specifically the part about a device.

---

[8]www.fda.gov/MedicalDevices/DeviceRegulationandGuidance/
UniqueDeviceIdentification

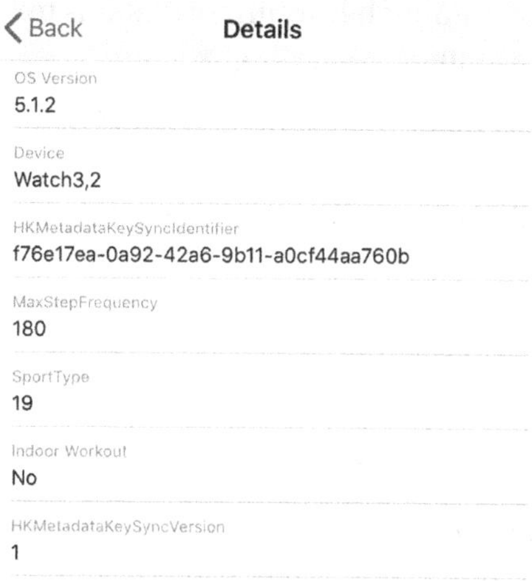

Figure 6-5. *The details of the device that recorded the data, and a few very nerdy metadata keys*

Passing nil is the way for HealthKit to know it will use the local device where the code is running. You can get that same device with HKDevice. local(). Alternatively, you can pass your own object describing potentially a Bluetooth device your company builds. Note that data can also always be entered manually via the Health app.

Deleting Objects

What is probably the third thing forgotten in most apps after security and testing? It could be deleting and/or cleaning data.

Either when the user asks you to do so, or when you technically need to do (e.g., to migrate to a newer API), you have a few different options in your toolbox.

Listing 6-6 shows a couple of different methods; especially the last one is crucial because it's efficient, because we don't have to query for the objects previously but simply pass a predicate.

I cannot emphasize enough how important it is to have an option in your UI that gives the ability to delete stuff. This isn't only a good-karma approach, but this will definitely build up trust between you and your user.

Listing 6-6. The Different Methods, Without Going Too Much into the Usage Detail

```
HKHealthStore().deleteObject
                .deleteObjects
                .deleteObjectOfTypes
```

They might never use it, and you are free to remember that deleting some data will mean your app won't be able to display the same level of information, but at least the option shouldn't be left aside.

Know Which Objects Were Deleted

Because HealthKit — as with many other examples like the Contacts API — uses a central database shared by all other apps (also the Health app, itself), you should be prepared for some objects being deleted in your back.

To that purpose, there's an API in HKAnchoredObjectQuery that has a list of HKDeletedObject in its resultsHandler. That handler can also be specified separately, at which point that query will keep running and the handler will be called when further samples are deleted in the future.

Note that — to save space — those deleted objects are only persisted for a limited amount of time, as mentioned in *What's New in HealthKit*.[9]

---

[9]https://developer.apple.com/wwdc15/203

Of course, it would be great if you could be notified when a specific object was deleted, since it might not be your code doing it. Well, throw your hands up in the air; there's a very handy function called enableBackgroundDeliveryForType that does exactly that.

You probably want to closely follow those types that are used to display data on your UI. Beware, though, that this is not available on Apple Watch. Speaking of which...

HealthKit on watchOS

More and more of the API set from Apple is becoming available with the same method signatures on multiple, if not all, of their platforms.

HealthKit is only half on iOS (because it's not on iPad), but on watchOS it has the same APIs as iOS — or I should say iPhone.[10]

Because of performance though, only a limited amount of historical data will be available on the Watch.

Requesting Access

The requests are made on the Phone, not the Watch. Imagine a small authorization UI on the Watch; that wouldn't make a lot of sense.

This is why, as you can see on Figure 6-6, the Watch will only display a message that can be dismissed, while the Phone will display a way to dismiss the message or open your app.

The authorizations themselves are shared — your watch will see everything your Phone sees and the other way around.

---

[10]Oh, look, Health is even available on iPod touch: https://support.apple.com/en-us/HT203037

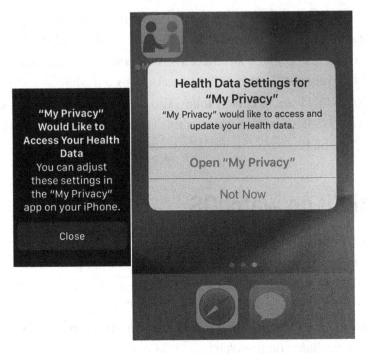

Figure 6-6. *Allowing access to HealthKit always happens on the Phone*

The data saved on the Watch (for example, when you're out for a Workout without your Phone) will then be synchronized.

There is a very good talk called *App Extension Best Practices*[11] from the 2015 WWDC, given by Sophia Teutschler and Ian Baird. In this, they show you that you should create an app framework with shared code between the extension and the app.

For the purpose of simplicity I added the class HealthManager to both Targets in Xcode instead, but their approach is definitely better — but also out of scope for this book.

---

[11]https://developer.apple.com/wwdc15/224

Listing 6-7 shows the call that will be received by the iPhone app when tapped. Mind you that tapping *Close* on the Watch doesn't do anything (besides dismissing the dialog), the same as *Not Now* on the Watch not doing anything.

Listing 6-7. The Call-Back in Your Application Delegate When "Open" Is Tapped

```
func applicationShouldRequestHealthAuthorization(
                        _ application: UIApplication) {

  HKHealthStore().handleAuthorizationForExtension {
                                    (success, error) in
    // In bad cases, report in the UI…
  }
}
```

Fitzpatrick Skin Type

If you are like me, you might have wondered why Apple provides six different variations of many emojis. It's not only Apple, it's a standard emoji variation.

The first one, yellow, isn't real (and comes from the original yellow emoticons) but the five others are actually medically real.

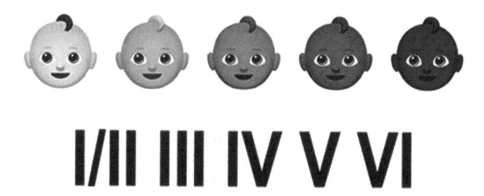

117

Those cute babies have five different skin types, or actually six, but the emoji representation groups I and II skins are relatively similar.[12]

The Fitzpatrick scale[13] uses a different way of computing your resistance to UV light. By asking you a series of questions, you end up being classified in the Von Luschan's chromatic scale,[14] which is what the emojis represent.

There is a method `fitzpatrickSkinType()` that returns an `HKFitzpatrickSkinTypeObject`, which in turn has a single property `skinType` being an enum with value from 0 (not set) to 6, corresponding to the type.

The `UVExposure` quantity type is a good combination with it, because depending on those two parameters (one with which you were born, the other one being the timely exposure) an app can warn you.

The warning is a good thing. I'm concerned about the skin type itself, because even though it's technically not the same as your skin color, not everyone would want that kind of data to be on some database.

You see, protecting privacy here might also be protecting your user from a potential breach into your database that would allow a crazy team of racists to decide that they will gather data on some type of skin. This really isn't what you need, so I urge you to really only ask for access to that information if your app is related to anything that has to do with UV exposure.

It's also your job — our job — to educate users (e.g., people in your family) to not allow access to certain types if they feel it's wrong. Remember, they can always change their mind later in the Settings App.

I wonder if Apple would be critical of an app asking for this. I hope they'd look for a specific functionality in the app justifying the access to this personal data.

---

[12]https://en.wikipedia.org/wiki/Emoji#Skin_color
[13]https://en.wikipedia.org/wiki/Fitzpatrick_scale
[14]https://en.wikipedia.org/wiki/Von_Luschan%27s_chromatic_scale

Reproductive Health

...and for many couples who are trying to conceive and for many couples who are trying not to conceive, monitoring fertile times and understanding hormonal changes or irregularities is critical information.

What's New in HealthKit[15]

Shannon Tan iOS Software Engineer

Apple says this was the #1 developer request for HealthKit, back in 2015. In 2019, with the Cycle Tracking App on watchOS 6 Apple doubles down on that important matter.

I cannot think of anything more private than this, but it's important that Apple takes it seriously for many reasons, one being that a new life (or not) might be implied. You'll find various types like `OvulationTestResult` in `HKTypeIdentifier.h` — or, obviously, the English documentation. I prefer the headers, a lot of time.

Sexual Activity

While most of the previous information is only relevant and private to the women entering that data, it gets even more private for a type like sexual activity, where the other person (if we are speaking about an identifiable relationship) is being tracked at the same time.

This is the problem of people letting an app access their contact database (in which you or I may be listed), but on a way more personal scale. Ideally, from a privacy perspective, the other person should always be asked.

To use that very low comparison of the Contact database, I would want to find a way for me as a user to hide my contact sheet to an app.

---

[15]`https://developer.apple.com/wwdc15/203`

In other words, this is **my** data and I want to keep it mine, and decide if people will implicate me in their decision to share my data — in the case of reproductive health, potentially, our common privacy.

Health Records

The Health app has had this feature since iOS 11.3,[16] and although in iOS 12.1 it was advertised as a Beta feature, the API for external developers arrived just after the front facing.

This is because Apple obviously needs third-party developers (e.g., hospitals and doctors) to fill in the database. Since iOS 13 it's not anymore described as Beta although still only available in the US, one can hope it will soon arrive to other parts of the world.

Since I hope we can trust our doctors and the health systems worldwide to be aware of the basic concept of privacy, there's hope this is going to be a very helpful technology.

One of the first things that will make you realize how different this is will be the authorization mechanism. HealthKit in itself is already different in that it has a very fine-grained UI for authorization (the dream of any of the other chapters in this book[17]), but the Health Records go beyond this.

---

[16]https://support.apple.com/en-us/HT208680

[17]To be fair, whenever there's at least a question (Yes/No) asked, this is already a win. I'm old enough to remember when any developer could read the user's contact list without the user even knowing. In 2019, in iOS 13, Apple also finally added a Yes/No for access to Bluetooth — and suddenly we all discovered a few Apps who had been using Bluetooth without the user knowing it.

Preparing Your Simulator

As a developer, the first thing you want to do is to avoid working with your personal device for everything. For Health Records this is especially true, but also if you are like me in a country where Health Records isn't available yet, Apple has prepared a set of fake/test data.

As shown in Figure 6-7, in iOS 12, you would do that by going to the Health Data tab of the Health app and tap the Health Records tab. On iOS 13 that changed a bit: You need to tap your Icon/Profile Photo on the top right, then Accounts, Health Records. The text before the "Get Started" button is a bit different in iOS 13, as well as the Location prompt. It's a perfect example of when you want to accept location only Once, since all it does is lookinf for hospitals in your surroundings. The first time, the setup process will appear.

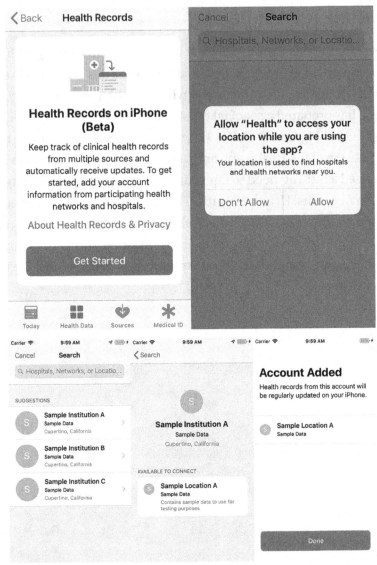

Figure 6-7. *In iOS 12: The process it takes to add a fake sample instituation and location; In iOS 13: As you can see Apple changed its color scheme and a bit of the introduction. Also you can see the new iOS 13 way of displaying modal windows as sheets with the view in the background shown at the top.*

Figure 6-7. (continued)

That location access, although well described (*to find hospitals*), is a bit of a privacy concern to me because — as you might have learned previously — there's no other way than the App Store Review process (brought to you by humans: those who can also miss a detail), for a user to know that it's only used for that.

After all, those purpose strings are just that: strings. None are really attached (strings) to what they really do. This got me thinking that:

- There should be an API to ungrant (or temporarily grant) access to the location. Hey, look, temporary grant arrived in iOS 13! Thanks, Apple!

- As a user, I would recommend in such cases to remove that grant just after the app has done what it wanted to do. That's a good trick by the way to get some apps working **at all**. That's the purpose of "Once" in iOS 13, but if you run an older OS, this is still a valid comment. Also, "Once" means the grant will stay until you leave the app. When you later return, you'll be asked again. As long as you are using the app, the grant is active.

Adding the Entitlements

First of all do not forget to add this capability to your app, as shown in Figure 6-8, by going into the Project settings in Xcode, in the Capabilities tab.

Capabilities: ☐ Health Records
Enable access to clinical data types.

Figure 6-8. *The newly introduced (in 2018, iOS 12) Health Records API*

Then you'll need to check `supportsHealthRecords` on your `HKHealthStore`. Listing 6-8 is what the console will report if you forgot that checkbox. At the end of the day, the only thing Xcode does when you click that checkbox is add information to your entitlement file.

Listing 6-8. The Console Output When You Forget to Add the Health Records Entitlement

```
[health_records] Failed to determine Health Records
availability with error: Error Domain=com.apple.healthkit
Code=4 "Missing health-records entitlement."
```

It's important to note that Health Records isn't supported in every region; if applicable, you should start by sadly telling your new customer it's not supported in their country.

This is where releasing an app only in certain parts of the world might make sense. Did you know your app doesn't have to be available worldwide, but you can fine-tune your distribution?

Also, as usual when it's a privacy subject, do not forget to set `NSHealthClinicalHealthRecordsShareUsageDescription` in your `Info.plist`. Otherwise, even though `supportsHealthRecords` will be `true`, the moment you try to `requestAuthorization` it will crash your app — but you should be used to it by now.

New Authorization Model

Apple is being very picky on privacy with Health Records — luckily. As Figure 6-9 shows, there's first a general Health Records panel, even before the types are shown. Listing 6-9 shows the way I'm asking for access to Medication, but as Apple says, it doesn't matter which specific part of Health Records I'm asking for; this is a very special case.

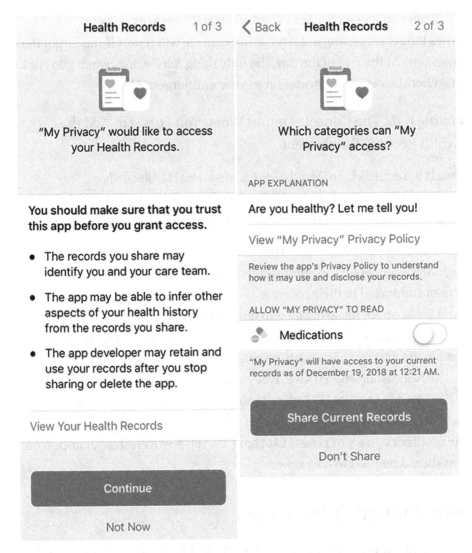

Figure 6-9. *The first step for general usage of Health Records and the second displaying the list of access request. This is how this looks under iOS 12.*

After the standard Health Records panel we present your authorization panel — this is your chance to explain [to] the user (thanks to the info.plist keys) why you need this access.

(...)

You should be sure that your request is proportional to what you need.

Accessing Health Records[18]

You might recognize that there's no "Allow all" button. Granted, here I'm only asking for one access, but even with more the user would have to go over each one. Figure 6-10 displays the last part of this process, where the user is given the choice to be asked each time new records are available.

---

[18]https://developer.apple.com/wwdc18/706

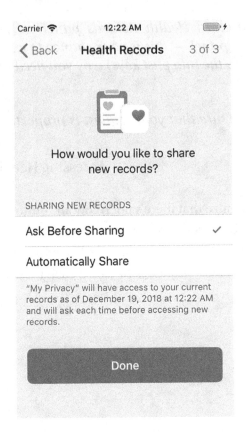

Figure 6-10. *The third part of the workflow, which asks the user about continuous access or not*

The single `requestAuthorization` call in Listing 6-9 will be that long the first time (3 parts, from *1 of 3* to *3 of 3*). That last part is important because you'll only be able to use background deliveries if the user has granted continuous access.

Listing 6-9. The Basic Request for the Medication Type

```
guard let medication = HKObjectType.clinicalType(
  forIdentifier: .medicationRecord) else {
    return
}
```

```
let store = HealthManager.shared.store

store.requestAuthorization(toShare: nil,
                read: [medication]) { (success, error) in
  let query = HKSampleQuery(sampleType: medication,
                            predicate: nil,
                            limit: HKObjectQueryNoLimit,
                            sortDescriptors: []) {
  (query, samples, error) in
    guard let sample = samples?.first as? HKClinicalRecord
      else { return
    }
    label.text = sample.displayName
  }
  store.execute(query)
}
```

Which brings me to the fact that as of now, you're dealing with regular HealthKit stuff, like HKQuery, for example. In Listing 6-9 I'm also getting those HKClinicalRecord that I'm authorized to query. In a very cheap manner I'm then displaying the first medication in a label — mostly to show you that you'll have to cast that standard HKSample.

The Full Monty

I'll get into more details later when speaking about the Argonaut project, but for the moment let me show you in Listing 6-10 what's actually behind that record. Apple extracts the nice displayName for you but it's also interesting from the privacy angle to see the actual/full JSON. You can simply get it with the other property on that object. It's a Data object, though, so you'll have to convert it to a valid JSON object, which is out of scope for this book.

Listing 6-10. The Full JSON from the FHIR (Fast Healthcare Interoperability Resources)

```json
{
  "status": "active",
  "note": "Please let me know if you need to use this more
                           than three times per day",
  "id": "24",
  "medicationCodeableConcept": {
    "text": "Albuterol HFA 90 mcg",
    "coding": [
    {
      "system": "http://nlm.nih.gov/research/umls/rxnorm",
      "code": "329498"
    }
    ]
  },
  "patient": {
    "display": "Candace Salinas",
    "reference": "Patient/1"
  },
  "prescriber": {
    "display": "Daren Estrada",
    "reference": "Practitioner/20"
  },
  "dateWritten": "1985-10-11",
  "resourceType": "MedicationOrder",
  "dosageInstruction": [
    {
      "text": "2 puffs every 2-4 hours"
    }
  ]
}
```

Get Request Status

Because you might not want to have an imposed UI always shown to you, Apple introduced a new API that will indicate whether your app needs to request authorization from the user.

It's not saying if the user accepted or denied, and Apple proudly reminds us of that. Listing 6-10 shows you how you avoid displaying the system UI directly. In essence, it's your designer-in-the middle attack...

The `HKAuthorizationRequestStatus` given can be

- *Unknown*: The authorization request status could not be determined because an error occurred.

- `shouldRequest`: The application has not yet requested authorization for all the specified data types.

- *Unnecessary*: The application has already requested authorization for all the specified data types.

This slightly begs the question whether this isn't already telling an app too much, but this is at the acceptable middle of convenience over strict privacy. Often refered as the sweet spot.

Listing 6-11. This Is a Way for You to Know HealthKit Will Present a UI

```
store.getRequestStatusForAuthorization(toShare: [],
                read: [medication]) { (status, error) in
  switch status {
  case .unnecessary:
      // go ahead with the query!

  case .shouldRequest:
      // maybe display your own "pre-UI" for explanation
```

```
case .unknown:
    // maybe you can add a retry button?
}
}
```

Furthermore, there's another way to "half know" if users gave access — or not — to a specific category. If you put these in the key NSHealthRequiredReadAuthorizationTypeIdentifiers in the Info.plist, the request will potentially fail with a new HKError: errorRequiredAuthorizationDenied.

Apple doesn't recommend you to use this, because your app should be able to work without it. They recognize cases, though, where you will need to know if the user decided.

The Argonaut Project

There's one thing that gives me a good feeling about HealthKit. That is that people from the medical industries are a big backbone of support behind it.

Users interact with multiple healthcare institutions over the course of their lives and these are often running different electronic health record systems that don't always represent data in the same way.

To address this the healthcare community came together in an effort called the Argonaut Project[19]; this uses FHIR, a flexible

---

[19]https://argonautwiki.hl7.org

JSON representation of health records and OAuth 2 as defined by the Smart Authorization Guide to allow connections, consistent connections to healthcare institutions and to allow data to be downloaded in a common format and related across those multiple institutions.

Jason Morley — Apple Health

Now that speaks to me. Also the fact that private companies like Apple will do what governments and politicians worldwide seem to not be able to do: uniformize data. It's out of scope to see if this system scales worldwide, though.

Don't Ask Too Much

When speaking about HealthRecords, Apple reminds us again that you should provide the user with information about how you store their data and you should provide a way for them to do delete it.

By any means, there's a privacy policy that needs to be somewhere on some website — and at best, directly in your app like Apple does with the Privacy logo.

Also, always ask for data proportionally: never ask for more than you need!

I'm Concerned About Preconditions, but…

While researching this topic, I was reading an article[20] that got me thinking about the ability for an insurance company to have a look at your records and determine preconditions faster.

---

[20]https://imore.com/health-records

Although they surely have an economic interest to do so, it also means they'll be able to get to that earlier.

It surely makes sense from a computer scientist point of view, but it's a bit frightening from a privacy perspective.

Then again — and let me be a bit polemic — a governments might decide they need access to your data. In general, this is why the technical side of things, and your ability to act as a responsible developer, isn't enough.

We need laws around the technicalities. There are many things we *can* do, like driving at 190mph, but we luckily have laws that prevent it, at least in most countries where sanity lives...

In Europe — and hopefully in many other countries soon — this might be in the form of GDPR[21] or another form. HealthKit and HealthRecords, like many other technologies, need to be looked into by politicians — in the hope that we find some who can somewhat understand the technicalities behind them.

I'm hopeful, as is this passage in the aforementioned article.

> *Being able to reach for your phone to share details of your last blood test or prescription list with any care provider is incredibly powerful. It makes their job easier, but it also puts you in control of the information. It removes obstacles like calling a busy office or worrying that the information was faxed to the wrong number.*

Health Records: Everything you need to know!

---

[21]https://eugdpr.org

Apple Doesn't Want Your Data

I was recently on the phone with Apple Support for a problem I was having with Screen Time.[22]

The Apple employee on the other side asked me to send a screencast of my problem so they can investigate. The first thing he told me was:

Please make sure you're not showing your password or pin code in the video. We don't want to see it.

I mentioned at the very beginning of this book that in a lot of cases you don't want to store the data on your site.

This is even truer when this data comes from another source anyway, like with the FHIR implementation.

Because we're on the subject of trust, here's a tip when writing your privacy policy or your purpose strings: Imagine that your user knows your app as well as someone working on it. Obviously not from a technological point of view, but from a data flow point. Explain in plain English — and/or other languages — where the data is stored, and remember: the less you store, the fewer privacy-related problems you have to deal with.

---

[22]This amazing technology allows you to control the time you spend on your iOS device, or the time your kids spend. Check it out at https://apple. com/newsroom/2018/06/ios-12-introduces-new-features-to-reduce-interruptions-and-manage-screen-time

Statistics

I'm unsure how much the word "statistics" itself is related to privacy, but I'm sure it is. After all, it's a completely different thing if an app knows how many steps I walked today compared with how much I walked in total.

Listing 6-12 shows what it would take for an app to produce this kind of statistic. It starts — in this case — with a request to access my steps count. It's important to note that statistics only work with quantity type, which sounds obvious. It's even more important to differentiate two kinds of quantity type.

- *Discrete*: You can ask for a min, max, or average, but it doesn't make sense to ask for a sum. Weight is a good example, where adding 7 days of my weight isn't interesting data. Note that Apple expanded the HKQuantityAggregationStyle enum to be more specific about Discrete as of iOS 13.

- *Cumulative*: They sum up. Steps count is a very good example. It makes sense to know how many steps I walked this week.

Listing 6-12. The Statistics That Retrieve the Sum of Steps I Walked

```
guard let stepType = HKObjectType.quantityType(
                forIdentifier: .stepCount) else { return
}
let qry = HKStatisticsQuery(quantityType: stepType,
            quantitySamplePredicate: nil,
                        options: .cumulativeSum,
                completionHandler: { (_, res, _) in
    if let sum = res?.sumQuantity() {
      let value = sum.doubleValue(for: HKUnit.count())
      DispatchQueue.main.async {
```

```
        label.text = "\(Int(value)) steps"
      }
    }
})
store.execute(qry)
```

Statistics Collection

If you want to show my average heart rate from the last week, this is when you'd use HKStatisticsCollection. This is technically a bit out of scope, but I wanted to mention it so you look at it deeper in the *Introduction to HealthKit* session from WWDC 2014 mentioned at the beginning of this chapter. Also watch the WWDC 2019 Session *Exploring New Data Representations in HealthKit*.

On the Mac

It's pretty simple: there's no HealthKit on the Mac. There's no Health app on the Mac. Move along, or move into the future, when Catalyst[23] might support HealthKit and the Health App will be ported.

Conclusion

With all the privacy concerns justified, I think it's probably inevitable that one day our doctor might retrieve our data with one click. That's okay-ish, leaks aside.[24]

---

[23]For now, as mentionned at https://developer.apple.com/design/human-interface-guidelines/ios/overview/ipad-apps-for-mac, HealthKit is one of the frameworks not supported — but neither is it on the iPad, btw, and Catalyst Apps can't be built from iPhone apps.

[24]https://www.mayoclinic.org/data-breach

Where it becomes more concerning is if this data is stored on some servers. Luckily, it's not on Apple's servers. Although one could argue it's better there than anywhere else, it's better when it's not duplicated. The more data (in this case your health information) is replicated, the more chances it has to leak at one point.

CHAPTER 7

Siri and Search

Apple has been working on making Siri better over the years by potentially using the kind of information you have in an app. Rumors of an offline version of Siri aside, we are still looking at a year 2019 where millions (billions?) of queries are sent to Apple servers.

The Machine Is Learning

Siri is more than the name of the voice that speaks to you — if you have it on at all. The ability to look/search in your app is the crucial part.

Never before in history have there been objects that know so much about us. About how we spend money.

About the emails we send, and the photos we take. About our messages. From our quickest hellos to our most intimate conversations.

When you think of it that way, you realize that protecting the security of all that information is so much more than just about technology.[1]

Ivan Krstić, Security @ Apple.

---

[1] https://developer.apple.com/videos/play/wwdc2016/705

© Manuel Carrasco Molina 2019
M. Carrasco Molina, *Karma-based API on Apple Platforms*,
https://doi.org/10.1007/978-1-4842-4291-9_7

The title of the paragraph doesn't mean I'll be speaking generally about machine learning or more specifically about CoreML and CreateML,[2] but you can imagine that analyzing some of your data can reveal a lot about you.

We give a lot of data to our devices, and although I personally rarely speak to Siri, I have to admit I do it more often lately and this is probably where the future goes. Now it's speaking, but imagine how it could be about watching (glasses or alike), or even thinking. I know what you're thinking: the year is 1984...

Suggestions

The first time I ran my sample app *My Privacy*, I was surprised to discover it in the *Siri & Search* item of *Settings* of iOS, as you can see in Figure 7-1.

The thing is, I had done nothing about Siri in my app. I didn't have that in the plan yet.

Figure 7-1. *The Suggestion part of Siri is on by default for all apps*

---

[2]https://developer.apple.com/documentation/coreml, https://developer. apple.com/documentation/createml — both of which have seen great additions in the iOS 13 SDK.

More particularly, I was surprised to read

Siri may learn from and make suggestions based on how you use this app.

I couldn't find a lot on what this actually means, and there's no precise "list all apps" settings or alike. Sure, it's convenient to say *launch XYZ* to avoid having to look for the *XYZ.app*, but this should be a different thing than *may learn*.

Access to Your App

The very first thing we'll show you in Figure 7-2 is that the first time an app is called from Siri, it will require the user to give access to their data.

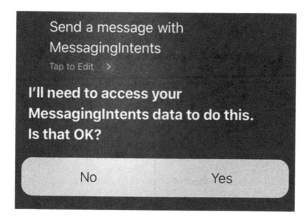

Figure 7-2. Siri will ask for permission to access your user's data the first time

Ask Again

As you might know, when permission is asked (e.g., to access the user's contacts or location), the app has only one chance, though this isn't really true anymore for location since iOS 13 and the "Allow Once" permission.

141

It means if I answer No to that question, Siri won't be able to access my app. That is reflected in Figure 7-3, and a user can change the value of this switch.

If I ask Siri again about sending a message, it will ask me again, and so it's like if the `UIAlertController` asking for permission for other APIs like contacts or location would show up again.

My guess is that Apple could argue that the user actually triggered this request, but tapping a button in a UI would be the same. The problem is that Apple doesn't have control over what you actually do with that button, whereas *Send a message* is clearly an intent first dealt from the operating system itself.

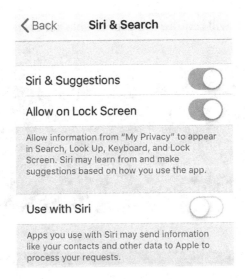

Figure 7-3. The setting Use with Siri is what is controlled by that previous question ·

That's the "I talk to Siri" part, but the two other switches are on by default. It means if you don't want those things to appear, you'll have to opt out.

From a privacy perspective I'd rather see a clear mention of that fact when someone starts an app, but we're probably back again in that discussion about usability. Imagine the nightmare if you were told about this for every app you start. Maybe Apple could tell it for the first three Apps started, for example.

Siri & Suggestions cannot be really turned off globally. You only have the option to turn that off app by app, which makes me sad. Of course you can globally ask to not see it in Search, Look Up and the Lock Screen, but does that mean it's actually turned off or only not displayed?

So what did I do or add at all to have this show up in my app? Here, I'm using Apple's sample app called MessagingIntents.[3]

Note Don't be confused where the sample code from Apple sometimes is. It's sometimes in a very handy location like `https://developer.apple.com/library/archive/samplecode/IntentHandling` and sometimes in a *.zip* file in a WWDC Session. There's room for improvement in their organization.

A New Capability

You are probably familiar with the Capabilities tab in the Xcode app target. As we see in Figure 7-4, turning this on adds the necessary entitlements in your app but also adds the feature to your app on the developer portal. That is an Xcode 10 Screenshot. If you use Xcode 11, you'll have to click on "+ Capability" on the top left of the "Signing & Capabilities" tab. Don't look for the On/Off Switch and also not for the Steps.

Then, by following the steps in the corresponding WWDC session you'll find that you have to add an extension and the corresponding code, which partly looks like Listing 7-1.

---

[3]`https://github.com/doronkatz/MessagingIntent-Sample-Code` is an updated version of the code written in June 2017, for Swift 3.0, from `https://developer.apple.com/wwdc17/228`. Someone might update it to Swift 5.1 by the time you read this book.

Figure 7-4. *Turning this on in your project*

There are many different intents[4] (and many are about your privacy) and the process of using a request made with Siri is always the same order of things a user/Siri interaction will look like.

It would look like Figure 7-5 if you didn't even configure your project to use that specific Siri intent you're asking to use.

Figure 7-5. *This is the standard answer that indicates that the app hasn't implemented the "Send Message" intent*

---

[4]https://developer.apple.com/sirikit lists some, https://developer.apple.com/documentation/sirikit all, although it's good to look at both pages to understand the conversion from the marketing to the developer language.

Before we dive into the three steps of generally processing an intent, it's important to check some intents we have at our hands, API-wise, at the current state of iOS 12.4 and iOS 13 Beta 4.

- *Lists, notes*: Siri can write to your notes, add list items, and alike. It can, for example, use INCreateTaskListIntent.

- *Ride booking*: Siri might know where you are and by any means where you want to go.

- *Messaging*: Could request access to your contacts. We'll use it in our examples.

- *Photo search*: Obviously — with the number of APIs for searching and identifying photos — this is an intent you should look at very carefully before implementing it.

- *Payments*: Apps that support payment, like your banking app, know a lot about you. Because as a developer you are tight to Apple (it could be worse), you might have to "share" some information with them. Things like INSearchForAccountsIntents[5] have properties like accountType (Savings, Mortgage, …), for example.

- *Workouts*: The chapter about Health and Fitness discusses dealing with that very personal information.

- *Restaurant reservation*: I hope you don't book too often at the local fast-food joint; Apple might want to sell you an Apple Watch to help you take care of your health.

iOS 13 adds a Media Intent that allows apps to play Music, for example. There is also the custom intent, which we'll see later. Let's now look at what it takes to process those queries.

---

[5]https://developer.apple.com/videos/play/wwdc2017/214/?time=342

Resolve

The very first step(s) is for Siri to have all the information to send. INSendMessageIntentHandling, which is used by an app to send a message, will need to resolve the recipient(s) of a message as well as the actual message.

Listing 7-1. A Few Things That Can Be Done to Have iOS Reply to the User's Wishes. A Message Needs Two Pieces of Essential Info: to Whom and What?

```swift
func resolveRecipients(for intent: INSendMessageIntent,
                    with completion: @escaping
                  ([INPersonResolutionResult]) -> Void) {
  if let recipients = intent.recipients {
    if recipients.count == 0 {
      completion([INPersonResolutionResult.needsValue()])
          return
    }

    var results = [INPersonResolutionResult]()
    for recipient in recipients {
      let matching = [recipient]

      switch matching.count {
      case 2  ... Int.max:
        results += [.disambiguation(with: matching)]

      case 1:
        results += [.success(with: recipients)]

      case 0:
        results += [.unsupported()]
```

```
            default:
                    break
            }
        }
        completion(resolutionResults)
    }
}

func resolveContent(for intent: INSendMessageIntent,
                    with completion: @escaping
                    (INStringResolutionResult) -> Void) {

    if let text = intent.content, !text.isEmpty {
        completion(.success(with: text))
    } else {
        completion(.needsValue())
    }
}
```

From a privacy perspective, the first concern, this is where an app uses whatever permission you gave it.

Note that we don't develop matching, which shouldn't just be an array of one recipient but rather a function looking for either your local database of users or the system contacts.

Confirm, Optionally

This part is when your app (or I should say extension in this case) has all the information it needs to process the data, but it will still present that to the user to confirm it worked.

Listing 7-2 is dealing with an IMSendMessageIntent again, but this is applicable to other intents as well.

Seen from a privacy orientation, it's the only chance the user has to ask the system to not do anything. It's too late already for the extension not doing anything, though, because there's no obligation to do whatever the UI (or voice) says.

For example, I could be an app sending messages but would actually look for who's your wife and always send her a copy of any message you send. That would be interesting if you message your lover but there's someone else knowing in Cc, and you don't know it.

Listing 7-2. The Confirmation That Shows When Siri Is Just Between Resolving Your Query and Handling/Processing It

```
func confirm(intent: INSendMessageIntent,
             completion: @escaping (INSendMessageIntentResponse)
             -> Void) {
  let response: INSendMessageIntentResponse
  if messagesProvider.isUserAuthenticated {
    response = INSendMessageIntentResponse(code: .ready,
                                           userActivity: nil)
  } else {
    let ua = NSUserActivity(activityType: "login")
    response = INSendMessageIntentResponse(code:
        .failureRequiringAppLaunch, userActivity: activity)
  }
  completion(response)
}
```

You don't need to confirm, but you'd be surprised if you're about to handle your request and the user hasn't logged into your messaging app.

Handle

This is the actual doing of the action — like sending a message, creating a note, searching for photos, or what not.

In Listing 7-3 the Siri extension really does the requested job. Once it's done, an actual confirmation — this time not a question but an affirmation — will be shown or said.

Don't focus too much on what an INPerson is, we will see that later.

Listing 7-3. Describes the Process of Filling a List of Messages (Here only 1), with Them Always Having One Sender and One or More Recipients.

```
func handle(intent: INSearchForMessagesIntent,
            completion: @escaping (INSearchForMessagesIntent
            Response) -> Void) {

  let userActivity = NSUserActivity(activityType "search")
  let response = INSearchForMessagesIntentResponse(code:
                  .success, userActivity: userActivity)

  let handle1 = INPersonHandle(value: "steve@example.com",
                               type: .emailAddress)
  let handle2 = INPersonHandle(value: "+1-415-555-5555",
                               type: .phoneNumber),

  response.messages = [INMessage(
       identifier: "identifier",
       content: "I am so excited about SiriKit!",
       dateSent: Date(),

       sender: INPerson(personHandle:handle,
                        nameComponents: nil,
                        displayName: "Sarah",
```

```
                         image: nil,
             contactIdentifier: nil,
             customIdentifier: nil),

    recipients: [INPerson(personHandle: handle2,
                          nameComponents: nil,
                          displayName: "John",
                                 image: nil,
                    contactIdentifier: nil,
                     customIdentifier: nil)]

        )]
  completion(response)
}
```

That (Resolve and Handle, with most probably a Confirm in between) is all you need to do to have your app give an answer to

Hey Siri, Send a message to John using My Privacy.

Your App Has a Siri Menu... or Not

As mentioned and shown in Figure 7-1, even before having the intention as a developer to do anything with Siri, your app will be in the list of Apps in the main Siri & Search menu in Settings.

As for every subject of the privacy theme, your app also has dedicated authorizations listed in its own item in the Settings app. It means if you scroll on your Phone until My Privacy appears — as shown in Figure 7-6 — and tap, you'll have, for example, the Contacts authorization you gave already.

With Siri, you might see it — or not. I cannot yet find a pattern that tells me when it's there and when not. By any means, your app doesn't appear in the Settings list until you have done another request/authorization or asked Siri to do something, after which you'll have the question again like in Figure 7-2.

Settings
Maps
Safari
News
Siri
Photos
Game Center
Developer
My Privacy

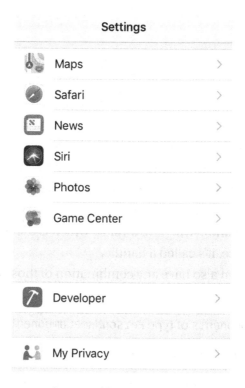

Figure 7-6. *That menu having the name of your app only appears whenever you either did a Siri request (and accepted) or you have asked for another permission*

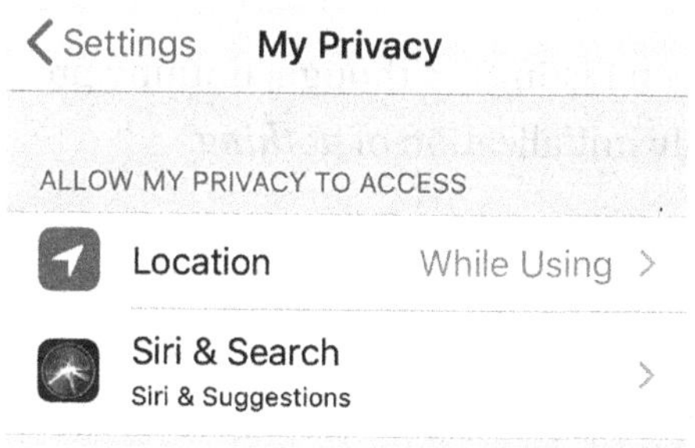

Settings
My Privacy
ALLOW MY PRIVACY TO ACCESS
Location
While Using
Siri & Search
Siri & Suggestions

Figure 7-7. *That Siri menu in the list of Privacy subjects for your app might appear or not*

Person

In the example of recipients, we're talking about the app internal list of Contacts and/or the actual system Contacts database, from the Contacts app. If so, an access to the contacts database will be required for references to it.

When an INPerson is instantiated, it needs an INPersonHandle. This, in turn, is instantiated with a type, which is either an emailAddress, a phoneNumber, or unknown. The INPersonHandle can have a label and a value — although I really don't see another use case than "single user apps." Usually this handle will have a value, which is the basic way you identify a user. Hence, it's called a handle.

The INPerson can also have any combination of those parameters when being initialized.

- nameComponents of type PersonNameComponents

- displayName is a simple string.

- image is an INImage, similar to a UIImage or NSImage.

- contactIdentifier is the string obtained from a contact's identifier. We'll discuss this later.

- customIdentifier is also a string for identifying.

As I demonstrate in Listing 7-4 though, nothing prevents me from doing that kind of silly initialization of *nothing*.

Listing 7-4. A Bare Minimum Initialization of An INPerson but Which Obviously Doesn't Make Sense. Some Combination of Those Parameters Needs to Make Those Users Unique, or Make Sense for the Task It's Meant to. If You Tried to Use This INPerson for Sending a Message, Obviously, It Wouldn't Work!

```
INPerson(personHandle: INPersonHandle(value: nil,
                                      type: .phoneNumber)
    , nameComponents: nil
      , displayName: nil
             , image: nil
  , contactIdentifier: nil
  , customIdentifier: nil)
```

A Connection to Your Contacts Database

Because your intent is a regular piece of code running on iOS, you can do all kind of things you shouldn't. One of these examples is that if you're going to call asynchronous code, you need to use a special technique telling Siri your request will need some time.

Another thing you should be careful of is anything that calls a system UI. Take the example in Figure 7-8. I decided — to be purposely wrong — to have a `CNContactStore().requestAccess` in my `resolveRecipients` method.

In this case, I asked Siri to *send with message to My Privacy*, which asked me to whom, and just after I said *John*, I got this UI. It's not only wrong because of the bad superposition of GUIs, it's foremost bad because the only UI for this request is a graphical one.

Siri didn't speak to me saying the app (in this case, really, the intent) wanted access to my Contacts, which means if I'm not looking at the screen, I won't know it.

Also, to wrap on this, if the user has said Don't allow — or if they change their mind afterward in Settings — you'll get a crash saying `[Rx] A promise was finished with a nil` error. Really, don't call this from your intent.

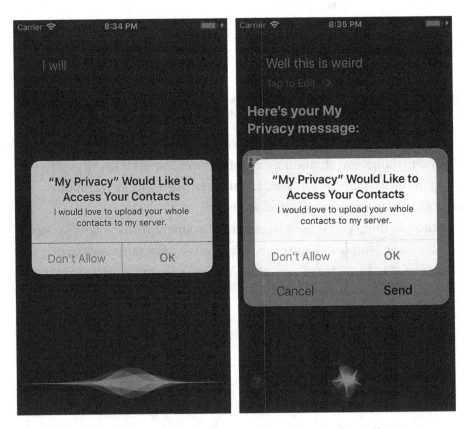

Figure 7-8. *Here is why you shouldn't have a request call in your resolve methods*

Instead I would recommend, as shown in Listing 7-5, to just check the authorization and return any of those two options, which are illustrated as the two results in Figure 7-9:

- unsupported, which appears on the left

- needsValue, which appears on the right

Listing 7-5. The Possible Acts When Looking for a Contact

```
if CNContactStore.authorizationStatus(for: .contacts)
                                    == .authorized {

    let pre = CNContact.predicateForContacts(matchingName:
                                    recipient.spokenPhrase)

    if let person = person(with: pre, for: descriptors) {
        results += [.success(with: person)]
    } else {
        results += [.needsValue()]
    }
} else {
    results += [.unsupported()]
}
```

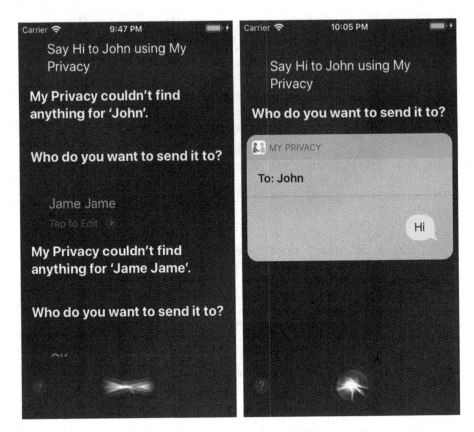

Figure 7-9. The two options you have when not finding a contact

The only problem I'm seeing here is that if I'm relying on access to the Contacts and the user didn't gave me that, I cannot find a way to say to the user that I can't find John because I'm not able to browse her contacts.

Potentially, Apple wants me to do this querying of the address book in the app and then I'd have access to an App-centralized list of contacts, but now let's look at what we **can** do when we have access.

Listing 7-6 shows you what a replacement for some of the code in Listing 7-1 could be, specifically in the resolveRecipients method. I also need a helper method that will translate a CNContact from my database to an INPerson, much like we did in Listing 7-4.

Listing 7-6. The Exclusive Usage of Fetching Information from the
Contact Database

```
var matching = [INPerson]()
let a = CNContactStore.authorizationStatus(for: .contacts)
if a == .authorized {
  let pre = CNContact.predicateForContacts(matchingName:
                              recipient.spokenPhrase)

    if let person = person(with: pre, for: descriptors) {
        matchingContacts.append(person)
    }
}

switch matching.count {
case 2  ... Int.max:
  results += [.disambiguation(with: matching)]
case 1:
  results += [.success(with: matching.first!)]
case 0:
  results += [.unsupported()]
default:
  break
}

func person(with predicate: NSPredicate,
            for descri: [CNKeyDescriptor]) -> INPerson? {
  do {
    if let contact = try
    CNContactStore().unifiedContacts(matching: predicate,
                                keysToFetch: descri
```

```
    ).first, let em = contact.emailAddresses.first {
    let handle = INPersonHandle(value: em.value as String,
                                type: .emailAddress)

    let image = contact.imageData == nil ? nil :
                INImage(imageData: contact.imageData!)

    return INPerson(personHandle: handle,
               nameComponents: nil,
                  displayName: contact.familyName,
                        image: image,
            contactIdentifier: contact.identifier,
             customIdentifier: nil)
    }
} catch {
    print(error)
}
return nil
}
```

Note that the displayName will now be used in the GUI of Siri. It means if you search for Kate, it will then display the image in Figure 7-10, because Kate's family name is Bell. You shouldn't rely solely on the address book access being given to you, but this is all business logic.

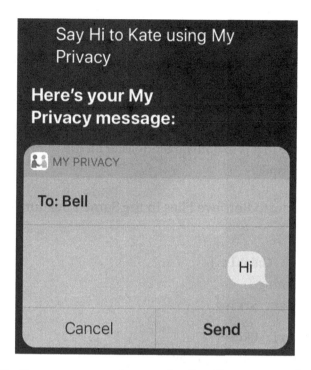

Figure 7-10. Because our code uses the family name as the display name, the request to Kate is translated to Bell

Also don't think that because a recipient/person/user is internal to your app you should treat it as less private, because you might have an app that people use for the good reason of not mixing contacts all together in their address book.

Saving and Retrieving Contacts

There are surely different ways of succeeding in this task and I speak about it partly in the chapter about Contacts, but as you might have understood, this chapter deals a lot with communicating from your app to an extension.

Speaking of which, there are many things you can keep here that are equally usable for other kinds of extensions like a Today extension, for example.

A Common Directory

You probably know about the Documents directory where you can save files that your app will have access to. If I wrote Listing 7-7 using this Documents directory, only your app, and not your extension, would see it.

This is a model class that I can put in a common framework (best option) or in a file that is in both targets (easier for the sample app; fewer things to understand).

Listing 7-7. How to Retrieve Files in the Same Location for an App Group

```
class Contact : Codable {
  var name: String
  var identifier: String

  static var url: URL? {
    let fm = FileManager.default
    guard let url =
    fm.containerURL(forSecurityApplicationGroupIdentifier:
      "group.com.carrascomolina.privacy") else {
        return nil
    }
    return url.appendingPathComponent("contacts.json")
  }

  init(with contact: CNContact) {
    name = contact.givenName
    identifier = contact.identifier
  }
}
```

Tip Use that containerURL in combination with activating App Groups.[6] These are some of the tips I got from watching the WWDC 2015 session *App Extension Best Practices*.

The beauty of the Codable protocol... Wait, I mean, of the Decodable and Encodable protocols, is that I can then use them to save like in Listing 7-8, which is in my Contacts View Controller, whenever a user selected a few contacts.

Listing 7-8. Saving the Selected Contacts to JSON

```
let encoder = JSONEncoder()
encoder.outputFormatting = .prettyPrinted7
var convertedContacts = [Contact]()
contacts?.forEach {
    convertedContacts.append(Contact(with: $0))
}
guard let url = Contact.url else { return }
do {
    let data = try encoder.encode(convertedContacts)
    try data.write(to: url, options: .atomicWrite)
} catch { print(error) }
```

This allows me to save the selected contacts in a JSON file like is shown in Listing 7-9. There are many ways to save records, and you should never store anything confidential (e.g., a password) in this text file, but gone are the days of using nonstandard formats for saving data.

---

[6]https://developer.apple.com/wwdc15/224
[7]This is useful for debug purposes, and my demo app really only is a debug app.

Listing 7-9. Contacts.json Saved in the Group Container Folder

```
[
  {
    "name" : "John",
    "identifier" : "410FE041-5C4E-48DA-B4DE-04C15EA3DBAC"
  },
  {
    "name" : "Kate",
    "identifier" : "177C371E-701D-42F8-A03B-C61CA31627F6"
  },
  {
    "name" : "Anna",
    "identifier" : "F57C8277-585D-4327-88A6-B5689FF69DFE"
  }
]
```

When Siri is being called, I then get access to this .JSON like in Listing 7-10, and I have a solution that works with or without authorization. In essence I augment the basic data that I recorded (here only the name) with the saved contactIdentifier, if the user gave access to the Contacts database.

Listing 7-10. Based on the Code in Listing 7-1, but Making a Few Changes

```
// (...)
if recipients.count == 0 {
    completion([INPersonResolutionResult.needsValue()])
    return
}
let coder = JSONDecoder()
guard let url = Contact.url else { return }
```

```
var contacts = [Contact]()
do {
  let data = try Data(contentsOf: url)
  contacts = try coder.decode(Array.self, from: data)
} catch {
  print(error)
}

for recipient in recipients {
  var matchingContacts = [INPerson]()

  if let contact = contacts.filter({
    return $0.name.contains(recipient.spokenPhrase)
  }).first {
    do {
      let name = contact.name
      let id = contact.identifier
      if authorized {
        let uC = try CNContactStore().unifiedContact(
            withIdentifier: id, keysToFetch: descriptors)
        matchingContacts.appendPerson(handleValue: name,
        displayName: uC.familyName, contactIdentifier: id)
      } else {
        matchingContacts.appendPerson(handleValue: name,
                displayName: name, contactIdentifier: id)
      }
    } catch { print(error) }
  } else {
    let p = CNContact.predicateForContacts(matchingName:
                                    recipient.spokenPhrase)
    if let person = person(with: p, for: descriptors),
  authorized {
```

```
            matchingContacts.append(person)
        }
    }
    switch matchingContacts.count {
// (...)
```

Note that I'm using a function appendPerson, which I added via an extension to Array where Element == INPerson. I'll leave this as an exercise, but you'll find it in the My Privacy iOS app as well.

Authentication!

All of this, until now, and by default, works totally without the user needing to log in. In fact, Apple's own messaging app on the phone can be used without any authentication.

Read that again... Grab my phone, start Siri (e.g., by holding the side button on an iPhone X) and tell it

Send a message to my wife

Now be creative with the message. If this isn't a security and/or privacy concern, I don't know what is.

I understand it's more convenient this way, and I don't think I myself would configure it another way.[8] There are ways to disallow this, but it's mostly opt-out, again, so this is quite tricky from a security/privacy point of view.

---

[8]As usual, feel free to duplicate www.openradar.me/46204420. I was pointed out the way to disable this in the past, but can you find it? See, it's not really obvious how dangerous this is.

How to Fix This?

Other than the user completely turning off Siri on the Lock screen,[9] it turns out Apple thought about this and offers a way for an intent to be Restricted While Locked. As shown in Figure 7-11, start by adding a new SiriKit Intent Definition file to your project then clicking the + to add a Send Message intent.

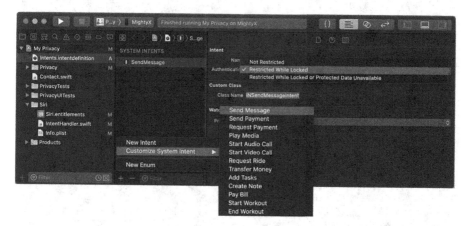

Figure 7-11. *This is how you configure an intent to not work while locked*

By default, there is no authentication required. Change this to Restricted While Locked.

The result is that you won't be able to use Siri to use your app (in our case *My Privacy*) without the phone knowing it's you. Figure 7-12 shows the two states in which this happens.

---

[9]Setting ➤ Siri & Search ➤ Suggestions on Lock Screen.

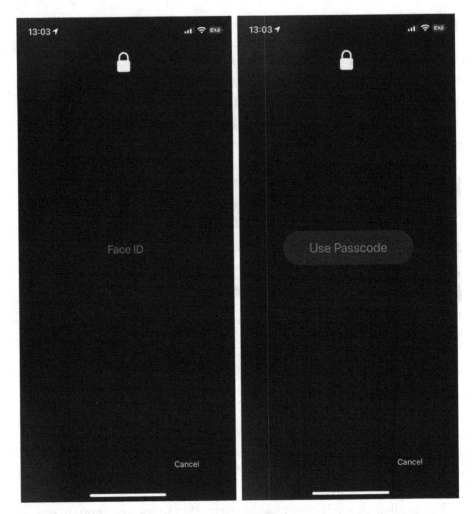

Figure 7-12. *If Face ID works, you won't be asked a Passcode*

First it was looking for my face, and then it still gave me the opportunity to enter my passcode.

There's another version of that unlock that I'm not willing to hide from you. It's when you restart and the phone needs your passcode to unlock, because Face ID hasn't been authorized yet. That, together with the result of the conversation with Siri, is in Figure 7-13.

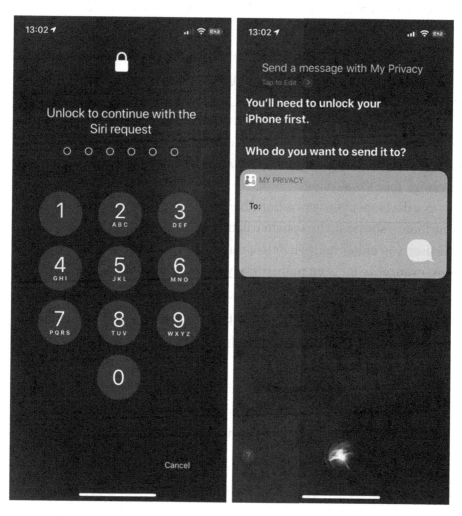

Figure 7-13. *First, a third version of unlocking. Second, the successfully unlocked phone*

NSUserActivity is Tracking You

The year is 1984... Okay, it's more like 2019, but there's a 19 in it! Seriously though, this is most probably what Apple really means with

> *Siri may learn from and make suggestions based on how you use this app.*

As mentioned at the beginning of the chapter, I'm not repeating this to grab your attention on one way developers can track their users, but for the sake of providing a feature.

When we look at shortcuts it will be clearer to you, but basically (and if the user allows it, but it's opt out, so most will), the system will look for a pattern. Talking about tracking you... This isn't the app developer anymore, this is the system.

As a developer you are responsible for the fact that however you contribute a shortcut, the system will try to find patterns in the user's life. As a user, you either refuse it or live with it. The third option is to read this book, evangelize for even more privacy at Apple, and file bug reports!

Yes, I often write bug reports that I later on realize I didn't understand the problem, but I prefer to write a few useless bug reports instead of not writing an important one.

Listing 7-11 shows the way to mark that a new page (or actually View Controller) of the app has been opened. It could do the exact same thing for when a button is clicked.

Listing 7-11. The Necessary Code to Mark That I'm Opening a New View Controller

```
let uA = NSUserActivity(activityType: "com.example.cont")
uA.title = "Privacy with my Contacts"
uA.isEligibleForSearch = true
```

```
userActivity = uA
uA.becomeCurrent()
```

We first create an NSUserActivity with a string that will be useful later. Then, we give a basic title that will be shown when searching in Spotlight. This is why it's EligibleForSearch.

That next line, where I assign uA to userActivity might be confusing if I didn't remind you that this code is in a viewDidLoad of the ContactsVC class of our sample app. You need to set this.

Finally, this instance needs to be current. As of now, as shown in Figure 7-14, whenever the user looks for the word "contact," they will be prompted with this searchable activity, which, mind you, isn't a shortcut yet.

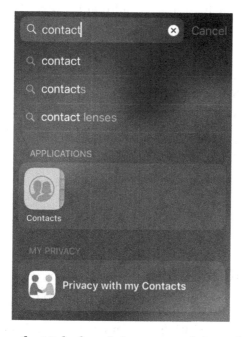

Figure 7-14. *Now that I declared the user activity, when I search for contacts, I can land directly there in the app*

Spotlight

Listing 7-12 shows how you can index data, instead of activities, or actions.

For that we'll use the Search API. We need to import CoreSpotlight for most of the code and MobileCoreServices only for that constant.[10]

Listing 7-12. The Other Way of Making Your App Searchable

```
let set = CSSearchableItemAttributeSet(
itemContentType: kUTTypeImage as String)

set.title = "Sunset with Privacy"
set.contentDescription = "August, 1999 Vimoutiers, France"

let item = CSSearchableItem(uniqueIdentifier: "1",
                            domainIdentifier: "album-1",
                                attributeSet: set)
let index = CSSearchableIndex.default()
index.indexSearchableItems([item]) { error in
    if error != nil {
        print(error!.localizedDescription)
    } else {
        print("Item indexed!")
    }
}
```

Proactive Suggestions

Depending on how you configured NSUserActivity (and you can even attach an attributeSet to it), the system will offer to not only hand off

---

[10]Thanks goes to Ellen Shapiro for her talk about Siri Shortcuts: https://vimeo. com/290292060

(e.g., if you have a webpageURL associated with an activity) but also offer to give you the directions for an activity having a location.

The example Apple gave in 2016 shows[11] the implications of it. Pretty quickly Uber will know about the location I was looking at in Yelp. It's not that those two apps or companies communicate with each other, but they speak to the same interface in the middle.

All they had to do was set the mapItem property of the NSUserActivity and voilà!

Spotlight, via its CSSearchableItemAttributeSet, can set a bunch of properties like city, country, latitude, etc., which you probably recognize from Core Location.

The Call-Back

So what happens when the user taps that link? Our app is called and lands in Listing 7-13. In the didFinishLaunchingWithOptions of the app I'm getting nc, which is a pointer to the main NavigationController in the app.

Listing 7-13. This Is Why the Activity Identifer Is Important

```
func application(_ application: UIApplication,
        continue userActivity: NSUserActivity,
            restorationHandler
: @escaping ([UIUserActivityRestoring]?) -> Void) -> Bool {

  switch userActivity.activityType {
  case "com.example.cont":
    if let nc = nc, let tvc = nc.topViewController,
    let vc = nc.storyboard?.instantiateViewController(
                        withIdentifier: "ContactsVC") {
```

---

[11]https://developer.apple.com/videos/play/wwdc2016/240/?time=820

```
nc.viewControllers = [tvc, vc]
    }
  case CSSearchableItemActionType:
    print("activityType CSSearchableItemActionType")
  default:
    print(userActivity.activityType)
  }
  return true
}
```

This allows me to directly jump to the *Contacts* section of the *My Privacy* app.

So *What* Is a Shortcut?!

By enhancing the code in Listing 7-11 just before we assign uA to the view controller's userActivity, we can provide a shortcut.

Listing 7-14 shows the iOS 12 way of doing this. As a reminder, I really think of this book for iOS 12 upward (ideally iOS 13), but if your app supports an older OS, you will need to use #available.

Listing 7-14. What Used to Be a Simple Activity and the Ability to Search It Is Now a Fully Fledged (and Standalone!) Shortcut

```
let uA = NSUserActivity(activityType: "com.example.cont"
uA.title = "Privacy with my Contacts"
uA.isEligibleForSearch = true
if #available(iOS 12.0, *) {
    uA.isEligibleForPrediction = true
    uA.suggestedInvocationPhrase = "Privacontact!"
}
userActivity = uA
uA.becomeCurrent()
```

Note that an activity needs to be eligible for search for it to be at all able to be eligible for prediction. The flag for prediction will be ignored if the activity can't be searched. I guess the underlying implementation of suggestions actually searches.

The result of this is shown in Figure 7-16. To reach that list of shortcuts you go into Settings, Siri & Search, as shown in Figure 7-15.

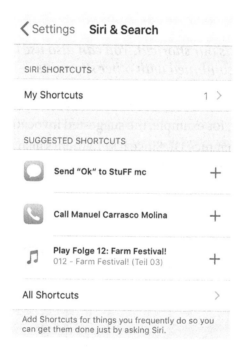

Figure 7-15. *The Siri Settings lists my shortcuts but also suggested shortcuts as well as the list of all shortcuts available*

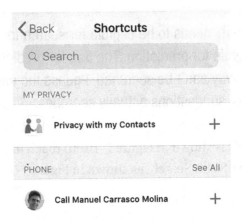

Figure 7-16. Here is our shortcut. You can also use it as a workflow in the shortcuts app, combined with other shortcuts

Now if you tap the + button, the Siri UI will appear and you the user can record anything, for example, the suggested invocation phrase. Figure 7-17 shows that nice UI. Since iOS 13 there's also a way to enter with text in addition to audio the "trigger text" that is used for the shortcut.

Cancel

Add to Siri

Privacy with my Contacts

🧍 My Privacy

You can say something like...

"Privacontact!"

After you record your personalised phrase, Siri
can use it to tell My Privacy to run this shortcut.

Figure 7-17. *That "Privacontact!" phrase I had in my code now appears. Note that this is an iOS 12 screenshot. It's slightly different in iOS 13.*

Siri Shortcuts clearly learns about your habits, because that shortcut will never happen until I go into the part of My Privacy that deals with contacts.

A user might not want you to track them. So, because the system doesn't do it, consider asking the user if it's okay to track her, or at least indicate where this can be changed, by providing the ability to open UIApplication.openSettingsURLString.

The Siri Watch Face

Even the watch benefits from that. Look at the Siri watch face in
Figure 7-18. It's convenient that it remembers what (and potentially when)
I turned on some lights or made tea, but it's also a bit creepy isn't it?

So yeah, it doesn't know I made green tea, but I know what those 2
minutes are for. Now already there are cups that can analyze what you
drink, so the general question here is: *Do we want to live in this world?*

As someone stuck right between politics/ethics and technology, I don't
know. What I do know, though, is that we developers have a huge role to
play in respecting the privacy of our users.

Figure 7-18. *The Siri Watch face knows what I might wanna do
next*

It even predicts what's relevant for you based on your location. That
being said, note that the user can configure which datasource she wants.

Relevant Shortcut

The concept of a relevance provider is what starts it all, and I highly recommend watching the corresponding session from WWDC '16.[12] They can come both from iOS or watchOS. Aside from a different icon (if it's from iOS or watchOS), the user won't see a difference — also because the API is similar.[13]

From a privacy perspective, there's a good thing about those running from iOS: they can't use protected data. Protected data is a piece of information your app can only have when your phone is unlocked.

For those running on the Watch, it would be very inconvenient if you needed to unlock your phone (you might first need to find it!) before a Shortcut could be displayed.

An `INRelevantShortcut` is created based on the potential relevance provider. There are different types:

- INDateRelevanceProvider, with a start and end date

- INLocationRelevanceProvider, with a CLRegion

- INDailyRoutineRelevanceProvider, which is automatically determined by the system such as:

  - morning

  - evening

  - home

  - work

  - school

  - gym

---

[12]`https://developer.apple.com/wwdc18/217`
[13]Except for `WKIntentDidRunRefreshBackgroundTask`.

Once configured, the developer adds those by calling the method `INRelevantShortcutStore.default.setRelevantShortcuts` and the machine learning in watchOS will then present those to you at the right time.

As mentioned in the WWDC 2018 session, there's always a great benefit about many things on the Apple Platform, one of which is the on-device approach.

> *It's also worth noting that this model is secure and personalized to each user. All of our learning happens on-device, and we're building a model for each and every single user of the Siri watch face.*
>
> Josh Ford, watchOS Engineer

Deleting Any Trace

Spotlight

It is **highly important** that you don't forget to delete. For that, `CSSearchableIndex` has a few `deleteSearchableItems` methods that will take care of cleaning some parts from Spotlight's index.

It is **very important** for the respect of your users Privacy.

NSUserActivity

If an `NSUserActivity` has a `relatedUniqueIdentifier` (via its `contentAttributeSet`), it will be automatically removed when the corresponding item is deleted.

If your `NSUserActivity` has no Spotlight item attached, you can always use the `persistentIdentifier` property and the corresponding `deleteSavedUserActivities`.

You can also call `deleteAllSavedUserActivities` when, for example, the user logs out of your app.

Intents

Since an `INInteraction` object can have an identifier and `groupIndentifier`, you can user the methods delete with a specific identifier or `deleteAll`.

Public Indexing

Let's add yet another detail on Listing 7-14: another small eligibility. By using `.isEligibleForPublicIndexing` (setting it true; it's false by default, unlike handoff), a developer has a very good advertising method, as well as a good discovery method for users of an app.

Now that I've had you freak out, I can tell you this was explained in a very good manner when the Search APIs where introduced in 2015 at the WWDC.[14]

The way this works is that a hashed object is sent to Apple for public indexing of activities that aren't private to a user. Think of it as of a certain product of a catalogue from an online store. What you shouldn't set for public indexing is, for example, the preferences of a user.

Whenever a certain threshold (no numbers given, but let's imagine 1,000 requests) has been reached, Apple assumes this is successful enough to make it public to the other users of the app but also to people not having your app who can query something you've indexed publicly.

In our previous example of the store, it could be that rain jacket you're willing to search on the web, but hey, maybe *there's an app for that.*[15]

---

[14]https://developer.apple.com/wwdc15/709

[15]Or maybe it was on the iPhone 3G — https://youtube.com/watch?v=szrsfeyLzyg

Turning Off Siri

It might be a little bit extreme, but I do know people who turn Siri off, for various reasons. What I want you to read from Figure 7-19 is the part about deleting your information.

Figure 7-19. *How the user can turn off Siri*

Note that for this warning to appear you need to turn off both "Press Home" (or "Side Button" on the newer iPhones) and "Hey Siri." That by the way will need to be reconfigured if you turn it off, which really is a good hint at your data being deleted from the device when you turn it off.

Apps Using Your Data

Even if it doesn't always mean that a third-party developer has access to raw data, the OS doesn't need many of those accesses and so, depending on the user's level of privacy he solely determines, those apps might not have the data they expect.

Figure 7-20 shows you four examples of apps that have relevant information about a user and who can share that information.

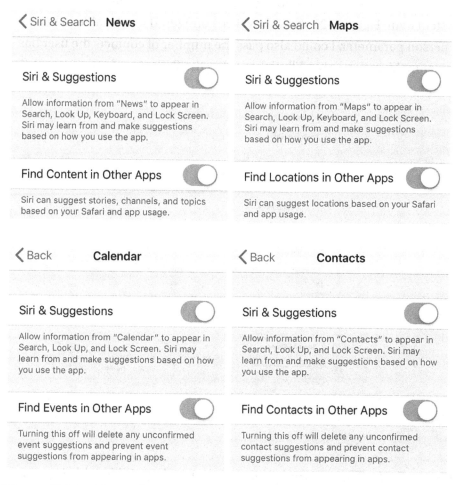

Figure 7-20. *The inclusion of some of the Apps from Apple*

INInteraction and Custom Intents

The Siri & Search APIs are pretty confusing, because they offer a ton of very useful technologies — although always frightening.

One of these is the ability to create custom intents. They won't have resolve methods, but they can have a confirmation and will need a handle, like any intent.

To create them, we should have an .intentdefinition file. In this, we'll add a new intent, instead of the previously mentioned customized system item. Figure 7-21 shows how I've configured it to be able to have a person parameter. I could also pass the number of contacts the user has — or anything else — but I'll stick to using the INPerson class.

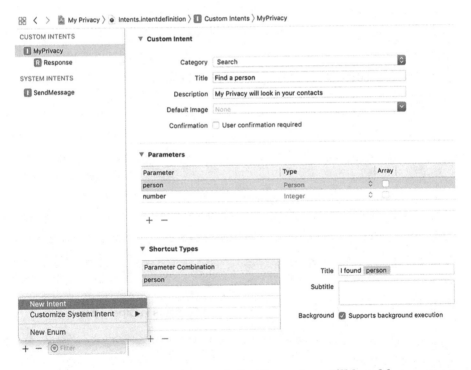

Figure 7-21. *The custom intent definition where I'll be able to pass a person*

Once this is done, as shown in Listing 7-15, we have the ability to create an interaction that has an implied user activity. This is a piece of code I could run every time the user picks a contact from the corresponding `contactPicker:didSelect contact` method:

Listing 7-15. The Code That Will Generate a Shortcut — Independent as Well

```
let intent = MyPrivacyIntent()
let pH = INPersonHandle(value: contact.identifier,
                        type: .unknown)

intent.person = INPerson(personHandle: pH,
                     nameComponents: nil,
                        displayName: contact.familyName,
                              image: nil,
                  contactIdentifier: contact.identifier,
                   customIdentifier: nil)

INInteraction(intent: intent,
            response: nil).donate(completion: nil)
```

Beware that this code needs to be running only on iOS 12 or later so you need to use #available if your app still runs on older OSes. If it's a new app you're starting after August 2019, you really should start with iOS 13 support, nothing earlier. This will automatically produce a shortcut that can be used. Using/calling this shortcut will then call our Siri extension and the code in Listing 7-16. It shows that the times where intents were just those defined by Apple are gone.

Listing 7-16. The Custom Intent with which We Can Do Custom Things

```
func handle(intent: MyPrivacyIntent, completion:
@escaping (MyPrivacyIntentResponse) -> Void) {

    // Do something with the intent.

    let response = MyPrivacyIntentResponse(code: .success,
                                    userActivity: nil)

    completion(response)
}
```

Because we didn't ask for any confirmation (checkbox unchecked in Figure 7-21), calling this (e.g., with a short phrase) would execute it in the background; no need to open your app.

The user can still open your app, though, by tapping on the app icon or the shortcut banner. This will simply send him to the aforementioned `application: continue userActivity: restorationHandler:` method in your App Delegate.

The little piece of magic here is that you will have a user activity that has an activityType of "MyPrivacyIntent" (the string derived from the class name) but as I'm showing you in Listing 7-17, you could even spare using this string checking.

Listing 7-17. Retrieving the Intent from the Activity's Interaction

```
if let intent =
  userActivity.interaction?.intent as? MyPrivacyIntent {
    print(intent.person ?? "no person found")
}
```

Contact Integration

If you have a messaging or video/audio app you can integrate directly in the Contacts app by using a similar code to Listing 7-18, based on Listing 7-15. It basically declares your service to the system. An app that does this should ask the user if it's okay to be integrated in the Contacts app, but there's no API for asking.

Listing 7-18. How to Integrate with the Contacts App

```
let mI = INSendMessageIntent(recipients: [intent.person!],
                                 content: nil,
                       speakableGroupName: nil,
                  conversationIdentifier: nil,
                             serviceName: "PrivzApp",
                                  sender: intent.person)

let response = INIntentResponse()
let interaction = INInteraction(intent: mI,
                              response: response)

interaction.direction = .outgoing

interaction.donate { (error) in
    print(error ?? "no error")
}
```

AppleBot

Although Apple might not yet be like Google in terms of searches, I like the fact that they describe this very well in the Session *Making the Most of Search APIs.*[16]

This is more a job for web developers or admins than mobile developers, but with server-side Swift arising, it might be a job for you as well. Check what is sent to bots, in general, and be sure it's nothing private to a user.

Independently from the privacy subject, I'm always concerned when search engines recommend something. It's really hard to tell how much of this is actual math and how much is marketing.

Speaking of search engines, if besides being interested in privacy you're also interested in protecting the environment (two very ethical subjects), you might want to use Ecosia[17] as your default search engine. They don't track you and they plant trees. I have no other interest in promoting them other than the purpose of this book: karma. When I speak about the subject of privacy in public, I subtitle my talk "A look at the karma-oriented APIs.". I was pleasantly surprised when Apress decided it was going to be the main Title of this book, not the original way around.

On the Mac

You and I got lucky lately, when it comes to speaking of iOS and macOS. If I'd have done the same book a few years ago, it would be double the size. You'd want to make an app for both, double the amount of time. Since the project Catalyst in iOS 13 and macOS 10.15, it's even less work because you can make a lot of your iPad app working on the Mac.

---

[16]https://developer.apple.com/wwdc16/223

[17]https://ecosia.org. Over 60 million trees planted just with search requests.

Spotlight is yet another API that is similar on the Mac and on iOS. Hooray! The code in Listing 7-12 is absolutely similar and as you can see in Figure 7-22, when I type the phrase that I indexed, it shows up in the category "Images". Clicking on it will open the Mac app, obviously, with an activityType com.apple.corespotlightitem, which is defined by the constant CSSearchableItemActionType.

Figure 7-22. *The Spotlight User interface which reacts to the contact in the Searchable Item*

Without going too much into the details, much of what there is in NSUserActivity is also similar, although there are no shortcuts per se on macOS, for example.

Conclusion

When I started working on this chapter, I thought it would be hard to write 10 pages about Siri & Search. I was wrong; so wrong. You could write a whole book about it. You could write a whole book about privacy with Siri.

Many people think of the term UI as something graphical, visual. That would be a GUI. Siri, mostly the audio version of it, is a fully fledged UI. The way you use your Watch in combination (or not) with AirPods is a UI. You can even imagine a scaled down version of the Watch (without the visual elements like the screen) in your earpiece, or say, in the box where you charge your headphones.

Sure, this is convenient. Sure, we're helping the user with app shortcuts like the Vision framework can recognize eyes and mouth, or CoreML can tell if it's me or my wife in a picture.

But I won't hide that I am a bit concerned about where this could all lead. I trust Apple, and I'm happy they're almost not in the business of making money out of data, but there's always a concern that this data could leak at some point and could be used to target some people.

The key thing to take away here is that most of the code runs on the device and the parts that are sent to Apple are encrypted and by any means anonymized.

CHAPTER 8

HomeKit

Ever since I was a kid I've been dreaming of home automation. Back in the day (I'm the Commodore 64 generation, which should tell you my age) it was only thinkable if you had a lot of money.

Nowadays it's not cheap, but it's also not impossible to afford. But my dream has evolved, in many ways. Sure, I do have some home automation, but I'm also concerned about something I wouldn't even think of in the past.

Potentially it's because we now call it IoT (Internet of Things), and in the 80s, at our level, there were a lot of things but no Internet. The gist of this introduction is that a smart home — in terms of privacy — isn't such a big deal as long as it's not connected.

Smart Hack?

This brings me to another kind of introduction. For the second year in a row I was at the Chaos Communication Congress. This is an annual event since 1984 (no kidding, they really started that year), organized by the Chaos Computer Club in Germany.

Among other things, it's a conference about security, but it's also a very practical one where there's as much soldering as programming happening. There was a session called "Smart Home, Smart Hack."[1] It was sadly in German, but the conference always provides audio translation in English.

---

[1]https://vtrust.de/35c3

© Manuel Carrasco Molina 2019
M. Carrasco Molina, *Karma-based API on Apple Platforms*,
https://doi.org/10.1007/978-1-4842-4291-9_8

At this moment I have no confirmation from either Apple[2] or the author of this talk that these kinds of privacy concerns would happen on a certified HomeKit product.

This is important because it goes to show you what is feasible, and why I can totally imagine some companies giving away smart light bulbs for free in the future.

Lights, Camera, Action

Well, actually, it's more like *light bulb, garage door, door lock*. These were the first accessories that Apple supported in HomeKit in 2014 when they announced it.[3]

The only reason I mention it is to make you take in account everything they support nowadays (mid 2019 is when I write this). It's actually impressive,[4] and also frightening, considering the fact that you can reach all of these remotely.

Remotely?

Yes, if you have what Apple calls a Home hub, then it doesn't matter where you are in the world; as long as one of these hubs is online, you'll be able to open your door, turn on your lights, or make the room warmer.

---

[2]`https://twitter.com/StuFFmc/status/1085581546092924928`

[3]Introducing HomeKit, which was at `https://developer.apple.com/wwdc14/213` seems to have been removed from Apple's website. I guess Apple now only wants you to watch `https://developer.apple.com/wwdc18/231` although there's a "What's New in HomeKit" Session from WWDC 2015, 2016 and 2017. I usually watch the videos from the beginning and then watch the "What's New" from the years after. There was no session about HomeKit in 2019.

[4]`https://apple.com/ios/home/accessories`

A hub is either an Apple TV,[5] an iPad, or a HomePod. The iPad sure is mobile, but it's more likely to stay home than your phone and there are more people with an iPad than the two other devices.

I don't know about you, but I turn off my Apple TV with a hard power switch when I don't use it, and I don't have a HomePod, so for me the iPad would be doing this.

Figure 8-1 shows the Mac version of the Home app where the settings of a Home also show which Hubs are present. See, I do not kid you; my Apple TV (Living) is turned off, but sure enough my iPad isn't.

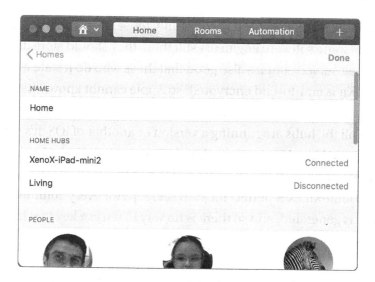

Figure 8-1. *The hubs used are listed in the settings of your Home*

---

[5]Starting with the 3rd generation, that's the thin one just before the fat one with apps arrived.

Note that HomeKit is one of four apps that Apple brought in 2018 from iOS to the Mac. It uses a technology called Catalyst, which brings UIKit to the Mac. The apps are very similar to their iPad version and when you resize your window they become similar to the iPhone version.

End-to-End Encryption

It blows my mind that we have to constantly repeat this, and that apparently some software engineers still think they should store decrypted data on their servers, but it's also good that those who do it state it.

HomeKit is end-to-end encrypted[6] so Apple cannot know what your setup is. The communication happens between a device and an accessory, and since all the hubs are running a version or another of iOS, it's surely the same code base. No cloud needs to be involved, since the Internet is solely used to transport the encrypted commands.

Also, HomeKit uses perfect forward secrecy[7]: for every communication, a new key is generated, and so there is no way to reuse a key that has been used and it's useless to save a key for a future use.

Finally, the keys are local to the device, so it's completely private and secure. I always breathe easy when I hear that nothing is saved on a server. It's much more complicated for a bad person to attack every single user of a platform — especially iOS, secured by things like sandboxing — than attacking a server that has centralized all the information for all the users.

[6]https://en.wikipedia.org/wiki/End-to-end_encryption
[7]https://en.wikipedia.org/wiki/Forward_secrecy

The Key and the Permission

The privacy key you need in your Info.plist is called
NSHomeKitUsageDescription, and you will then get a prompt asking you in
a very simple *OK/Don't allow* manner.

By now you probably understand the mechanism behind it: the String
in your plist will be displayed to the user, your app will crash without it,
and nothing will be doable if the user revokes his allowance at a later time.

The Home Manager and Simulator

Most of us only have one home, but many have either an office they also
control or potentially a holiday home.

Listing 8-1. A Basic HomeManager

```
import HomeKit

class HomeVC: PrivacyVC, HMHomeManagerDelegate {
  let manager = HMHomeManager()

  override func viewDidLoad()
  {
    super.viewDidLoad()
    manager.delegate = self
  }

  func homeManagerDidUpdateHomes(_ manager: HMHomeManager)
  {
    print(manager.homes)
    print(manager.primaryHome ?? "no primary home")
  }
}
```

Speaking of managing your home, you don't have to buy every HomeKit device to start developing for HomeKit. You can use the HomeKit Simulator (shown in Figure 8-2) if you manage to find it...

Xcode gives this weird URL,[8] which is like finding a needle in a haystack and the documentation[9] sadly doesn't gives a better information. In it there's a link *Testing Your App with the HomeKit Accessory Simulator*[10] which sends to the same needle.

Optionally in the browser, you can simply search for "HomeKit" and download the "Additional Tools for Xcode" .dmg file. Keep in mind this Home Kit Simulator is there.

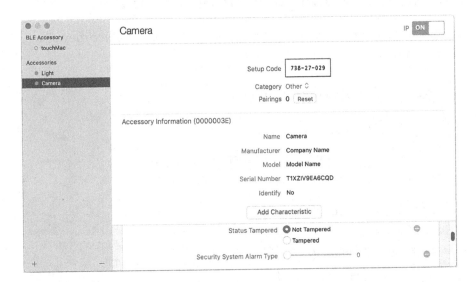

Figure 8-2. *The HomeKit Accessory Simulator from the comfort of your Mac*

---

[8]https://developer.apple.com/download/more/?=for%20Xcode

[9]https://developer.apple.com/documentation/homekit

[10]https://developer.apple.com/documentation/homekit/testing_your_
  app_with_the_homekit_accessory_simulator

Name Your Home

Let me show you in Listing 8-2 one simple way I'd ask a user to name her home. Please, oh please, do not ask with Core Location where the house is, as this is not of interest for you. The user knows where she lives. You could provide it as an alternative, but in most cases a simple string for the name is enough.

Listing 8-2. A Simple Approach to Asking for a Name for Your Home

```
func homeManagerDidUpdateHomes(_ manager: HMHomeManager) () {
  if manager.homes.isEmpty {
    alert = UIAlertController(title: "Name your Home",
                              message: "I suggest `Home`...",
                                text: "Home",
                              action: "OK") {
      let name = self.alert?.textFields?.first?.text
        self.manager.addHome(withName: name ?? "<home>",
                  completionHandler: { (home, error) in
            print(error ?? "no errors")
            if let home = home, errors == nil {
                self.whatsInTheRoom(home)
            }
        })
    }
    if alert != nil {
        present(alert!, animated: true, completion: nil)
    }
  }
}
```

The result of this code is shown in Figure 8-3. As you might have guessed, I have a little extension UIAlertController behind the scenes. You can find it in the source code of the sample app.

Figure 8-3. *The My Privacy app asks for a home name when it doesn't find one*

HomeKit itself doesn't provide a way to attach a home to a location, but obviously you could easily do it with either extending or compositing with HMHome. As always, just because you *can* doesn't mean you should.

Rooms and Accessories

If you are lucky enough to have a home with more than one room, you'll be happy to learn you can assign the accessories to different rooms. By default, though, the Home app will create a Default room, but you can always add a room with addRoomWithName.

Let's Browse!

A room has accessories, or, actually, we should say that a home has accessories, since it's at that level that you can work. There is, however, an array of accessories for a room, as well as a pointer from the accessory to the room it belongs to.

Listing 8-3 shows you how you should browse for devices that aren't yet added to your home. It's a process that one of the apps connected to the shared database does. After that, all the other apps won't have to do it.

Listing 8-3. The Browsing Part of the Class

```
class HomeVC: UIViewController, HMAccessoryBrowserDelegate {
    let browser = HMAccessoryBrowser()

    override func viewDidLoad() {
        super.viewDidLoad()
        browser.delegate = self
    }

    @IBAction func browse() {
        label.text = "Browsing Accessories"
        buttonSwap(title: "Tap to stop",
                   target: self,
                   action: #selector(stopSearching))
        browser.startSearchingForNewAccessories()
    }

    @objc func stopSearching() {
        browser.stopSearchingForNewAccessories()
        label.text = "New accessory?"
        buttonSwap(title: "Tap to browse",
                   target: self,
                   action: #selector(browse))
    }

    func accessoryBrowser(_ browser: HMAccessoryBrowser,
      didFindNewAccessory accessory: HMAccessory) {
        print(accessory)
    }
}
```

People got the power. Consuming more energy than needed is a karma-less activity. Help me save our environment by using the right API, in this case stopping searching for new accessories. It's comparable to `stopUpdatingLocation` with `CoreLocation` — it's like a radio working when it's not necessary. Also, the user will thank you for not draining their battery. As a speaker at conferences one of the current talk I give is called "Save the environment with Xcode" where I discuss things like the Energy Organizer in Xcode or the Energy logs — these are tools that helps produce a better energy-optimized app.

HMAccessory

Listing 8-4 shows the result in the Xcode console that the `print` in `didFindNewAccessory` will produce, based on our configuration in Figure 8-2.

Listing 8-4. Our Simulated Configuration

```
<HMAccessory, Name = Light,
Identifier = F887C510-2FDE-5E31-B013-5216405FEE28, Reachable = YES>

<HMAccessory, Name = Camera,
Identifier = FBDC9FE0-98F5-59D9-BC20-14096F7375B7, Reachable = YES>
```

By now you should understand that an accessory is a physical device, assigned to a room (which can change). That accessory has a pointer back to a room and an array of services.

Let's see in Figure 8-4 what we can do with that found accessory. The warning about the accessory being uncertified will be shown as long as the hardware accessory hasn't been certified by Apple — it means in the simulator, always.

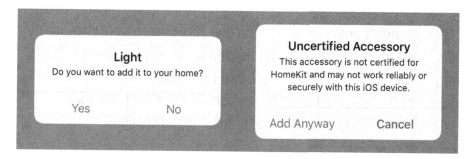

Figure 8-4. *The process of adding an element*

In an unusual manner for this book (I usually first show the code), let's now look in Listing 8-5 at what it takes to add the accessory. Note that it's added to the house, regardless of which room. This could be your chance to add a back reference to your home in a custom (probably composed) class, since HMAccessory sadly doesn't provide that back reference pointer.

Listing 8-5. A Way You Can Ask Your Users if They Want to Add Accessories

```
func accessoryBrowser(_ browser: HMAccessoryBrowser,
  didFindNewAccessory accessory: HMAccessory) {
    present(UIAlertController(title: accessory.name,
                          message: "Do you want...") {
        self.home?.addAccessory(accessory) { (error) in
            print(error)
        }
    })
}
```

That wouldn't scale for more than one accessory found, because by the time I'm in the call-back the second accessory has been skipped. In your real code you should save that array and process it at a later time. For us, because I want to only turn on/off a light, it's good enough — although I hate to say or hear "good enough."

Setup Code

So you think we made it?! Nope, and that's a good thing for your security, privacy, and foremost safety! We need a code, as shown in Figure 8-5. That dialog comes directly from HomeKit.

Only when the right code is entered will the accessory be installed.

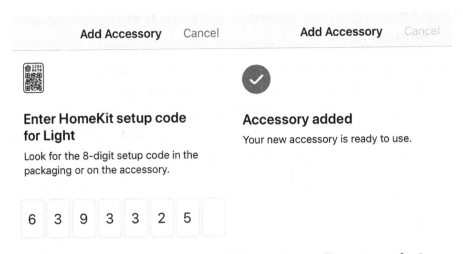

Figure 8-5. *The code you can find either physically on your device or in the HomeKit Accessory Simulator shown in Figure 8-2*

Listing 8-6 shows what happens in the console if I run a code showing me the rooms in my home and the accessories. The debug description of rooms isn't super exciting (just the memory pointer)

Did you know that whatever the console prints is the result of the implementation of either `description` or `debugDescription`? This is also why you really should avoid displaying a raw print of an object (simply represented by %@ in the ObjC days) to the user but instead use a property such as name.

And in the Real World?

For now we've only worked with the simulator, but let me show you what some of the accessories in a real home look like. Listing 8-6 is a more realistic representation of what a household might look like.

Listing 8-6. Printing the List of Rooms and Accessories a Home Has

```
[<HMRoom: 0x2817d0f40>, <HMRoom: 0x2817d7780>, <HMRoom:
0x2817cdf00>, <HMRoom: 0x2817ce700>

[<HMAccessory, Name = Philips hue - 01E807, Identifier =
43EEA8E7-62D6-56CF-ACF3-9CF2DB86E423, Reachable = YES>,
<HMAccessory, Name = Hue Dimmer, Identifier = E780B6AE-
9470-529B-B34C-2E599FEAFE9D, Reachable = YES>, <HMAccessory,
Name = Hue ambiance lamp, Identifier = EE1DAC3E-0FF7-541C-
9569-7A85C3D434B2, Reachable = YES>, <HMAccessory, Name =
Hue ambiance candle, Identifier = D96399D6-FF26-5EDC-A239-
855DF24A522F, Reachable = YES>, <HMAccessory, Name = Hue color
lamp, Identifier = DFDB4EA0-C7EC-57F5-B60A-A6C8B1A7B8F6,
```

Reachable = YES>, <HMAccessory, Name = Hue white lamp,
Identifier = 010AC899-F740-5952-B86A-443F852F639D, Reachable =
YES>, <HMAccessory, Name = FIBARO Single Switch , Identifier =
6E36D81F-1FA0-560D-A9EF-F9FB79E06906, Reachable = YES>,
<HMAccessory, Name = TJ HomeBridge-A964, Identifier = F2B84B60-
F6F4-570E-9DA1-1EAC02023C0C, Reachable = NO>, <HMAccessory,
Name = Fibaro Switch (#6), Identifier = 07AC997F-7244-5863-
93E4-DBCBE7AAC707, Reachable = NO>]

You can see there we have a couple of Philips Hue lamps. They are very
popular in the HomeKit world, but you shouldn't necessary go for them.
Ikea also has some, as well as most of the well-known light bulb makers.
What you definitely should do is your own research on the privacy of it. I
couldn't get a statement from Philips or Ikea about the "SmartHack" talk.

The reason I mention it again is that no matter how much security
and privacy there is on Apple's side,[11] the software/hardware/firmware
(accessory direct) sniffing data is probably the highest concern here.

Reachability

Before you do anything concrete with an accessory, don't forget to check
its isReachable property. Most lamps, for example, will be controlled by
a physical switch. If one is turned off, and you don't have something like a
Fibaro module,[12] you'll be out of luck.

Luckily, most smart bulbs nowadays remember the state at which they
were turned off, so if you dimmed it, when you turn it back on it should be
at the same level.

---

[11]I also don't really have a confirmation from them that they analyze the products
they certify.

[12]https://fibaro.com/us/products/switches — Bosch has a similar product
which I'm keen to try soon.

Finally, a word of warning about paranoia: you might be bitten by your own automation. So before you think a random hacker has taken control of your home, check if it's not your own rule that turns off the lights at 10pm every evening. Been there, thought that.

Services and Characteristics: Bluetooth Anyone?

If you've worked with the Bluetooth specs, or with CoreBluetooth, the concept behind services and their characteristics will be familiar. Speaking of which by the way, any app that requires access to Bluetooth will see an Authorization Prompt as of iOS 13 like with other authorization. That is a great addition for privacy that will make you discover which app is using Bluetooth.

Beyond an accessory being a physical device, there will be one or more services, and each one will have one or more characteristics.

First of all every accessory has an "Accessory Information" service, which simply identifies it. To explain the rest, it's always convenient to take the example of a garage door or a fan. Both of them have the obvious service to open/close or start/stop, but both of them might also have a light bulb.

You first need to define what you want to know: interact with the lamp, or with the primary service? Then you'll use the characteristics on that service to control the behavior.

Listing 8-7 shows the way I can turn on and off a lamp. If you know a bit about how Bluetooth works, you'll remember that characteristics are defined with UUID. Conveniently, HomeKit has a set of constants for it.

Listing 8-7. How I Browse the Services to Find the Bulb and Then Its Characteristics to Find the Power

```
buttonSwap(title: "Turn it on",
          target: self,
          action: #selector(turnOnOff))
```

```
@objc func turnOnOff() {
    let services = accessory?.services.filter {
        $0.serviceType == HMServiceTypeLightbulb
    }
    if let service = services?.filter({
        return $0.serviceType == HMServiceTypeLightbulb
    }).first, let power = service.characteristics.filter({
        return $0.characteristicType ==
                                HMCharacteristicTypePowerState
    }).first, let value = power.value as? Int {
        power.writeValue(value == 0 ? 1 : 0) {
            print($0)
        }
    }
}
```

Without those two constants (which will hopefully be part of an enum at some point), we would have to look for

- "00000043-0000-1000-8000-0026BB765291": Light Bulb

- "00000025-0000-1000-8000-0026BB765291": Power State

Imagine the nightmare of having to remember these. Also, from a privacy point of view this is already obfuscating the information a little bit, since it takes a little bit of knowledge to do something with them.

It's obviously not enough, since these are documented, but it means anyone wanting to read my home would not only need to have access to my device and let me install their app, but they would have to take the time needed to be familiar with those constants and/or this API.

Scenes and Automation

The power of home automation relies not only on acting on a single accessory but on grouping those not only in rooms but in Scenes, like the typical example of saying "good night" and all your lights turn off.

This is represented by HMActionSet. I really dislike it when there's a dichotomy between the technical term and the user language, but for now remember a Scene is an ActionSet.

Figure 8-6 shows a few simple Scenes that would turn off all lamps (Good night) where you can see that an icon has been chosen (not part of HomeKit, only of the Home app) and two others, which associates a few lamps together.

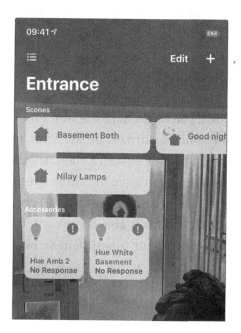

Figure 8-6. *The scenes associated with the entrance, although they really affect other lamps*

Automation wanted to bring the same dichotomy, so here is your new technical term to remember: HMTrigger.

Figure 8-7 shows the power outlet being "woken up" every morning so my wife doesn't hate me for the rest of the day.

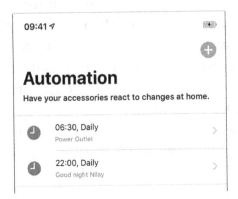

Figure 8-7. *The automation reusing a scene or acting on a single accessory*

User Management

You might not live alone; you might have a family, for example. So you'd want to give others the ability to turn on/off the lights, for example.

This is achieved with HMUser as well as HMHomeAccessControl. Listing 8-8 shows you the way to have the HomeKit-managed UI appearing in Figure 8-8. The cumbersome way to check if the currentUser is an administrator is also documented in this code. Feel free to create an isAdministrator function in an extension of HMUser.

Listing 8-8. The Way to Display the User Management UI

```
if home.homeAccessControl(for: home.currentUser)
      .isAdministrator {
          home.manageUsers { (error) in
                print(error)
          }
}
```

Figure 8-8. *The UI that will be shown once you call manageUsers*

Presence

Speaking of users, automation allows you to do things whenever the last user leaves home or the first arrives at home... This is a serious privacy concern because, if in the hands of the wrong people, this means the house is ready to be robbed.

I'm not going into the technical details of how this is being done because this is the less trivial part of HomeKit and this isn't a book about HomeKit, but I want you to know those privacy-involved possibilities exist.

Bridges

Many accessories out there use technologies that aren't directly supported by HomeKit. If it's not over Bluetooth or WiFi, HomeKit itself won't see it.

I can think of two off the top of my head: ZigBee and Z-Wave. The first one is used by the Philips or Ikea lamps, for example, and the other one by the Fibaro accessories. Both of them have a separate hub that then implements the HomeKit Accessory Protocol.[13]

---

[13]https://developer.apple.com/support/homekit-accessory-protocol

This is the same protocol that an accessory uses directly. This is also why you shouldn't see a *Works with HomeKit* logo on the accessory itself (bulb, for example) but only on the bridge, for some of the providers. For a user, it's a bit confusing — also the fact that if you have one bridge it can control all lamps, since it's the same technology.

One would hope that in the future Apple will support more technologies, by simply having the necessary component in *their* hubs. One of the reasons to use the other technologies is the range. Bluetooth isn't ideal when it comes to range. Apple has an idea about that...

Range Extenders

A range extender, as its name says, is here to help your hub or device reach a device that would be too far away.

The important thing to note here is that this accessory won't see any unencrypted data but rather just further send the encrypted packets, which only the final receiver will be allowed to decrypt.

Media Accessories

Although it's totally understandable to be worried about someone being able to turn off your lights or transform your living room into a sauna, the concern about privacy grows when an accessory has a camera and/or a microphone. Luckily in 2019 Apple announced HomeKit Secure Video — Check it out at `https://developer.apple.com/videos/play/wwdc2019/101/?time=2572`.

HomeKit has supported these since 2016. It can control many settings as well as display live stream and still images, so they'd better be good about protecting my privacy!

This is done with `HMCameraProfile` or `HMCameraAudioControl`. Please, from a privacy perspective, do not do anything that the user isn't informed about (e.g., do not record while showing a UI where you don't announce it).

Apple TV

Although there isn't a Home App (as in, a GUI) on the Apple TV, there's Siri, which allows you to do *some* things.

> *There is one major limitation: Apple TV and Siri Remote don't have Touch ID or heart-rate sensors to authenticate you the way iPhone, iPad, and Apple Watch do, so you can't control anything that requires authentication. That includes garage door openers or door locks.*
>
> *It might sound inconvenient but it's really about security. If someone gets ahold of your Siri remote and changes the colors of your lights, it's annoying. If they open your doors to intruders, it's potentially life-threatening.*
>
> tvOS 10 review, iMore[14]

The Apple TV — or I should say tvOS — does have HomeKit, though, so obviously a few solutions from third parties reconstructed the iOS & Mac app. It's interesting that Apple hasn't done it themselves.

Siri on iOS

It's important from a Privacy aspect to remember that Siri will know about your Home configuration, and it won't ask you that.

We can see, however, in Figure 8-9 that the section *Face ID & Passcode*[15] has a set of *Allow Access When Locked*.

---

[14]https://imore.com/tvos — https://imore.com/why-isnt-home-app-apple-tv
[15]If your device doesn't have FaceID, that will be another name.

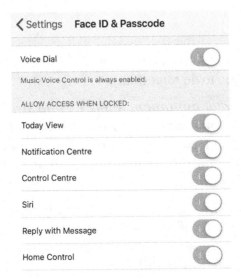

Figure 8-9. *Home control is one of these things you can decide as a user to be able to control with or without authentication*

It is therefore your responsibility to decide where you want your "convenience over security/privacy" level.

On the Mac

The very first image in this chapter was from the Mac version of the Home app added to macOS in 2018 in the form of a — as we now know — a Catalyst App. It's also called "UIKit for Mac" or "iPad App for Mac". You can imagine this app uses HomeKit itself, and so you can imagine... Well, no, I'm sorry, move along....

```
Macintosh HD > Applications > Xcode.app > Contents > Developer
> Platforms > MacOSX.platform > Developer > SDKs > MacOSX.sdk >
System > Library > PrivateFrameworks > HomeKit.framework
```

For now, as of macOS 10.14.6 Mojave or macOS 10.15 Beta 4, it's a private framework. Which brings me to the fact that Apple specifically mentioned HomeKit won't be supported in an iPad app running on the Mac.[16]

Figure 8-10 is a consolation for you since HomeKit isn't there yet — unless you'd like to play with private APIs — and shows the Home app. It's basically the opposite of tvOS, where we have HomeKit but no app.

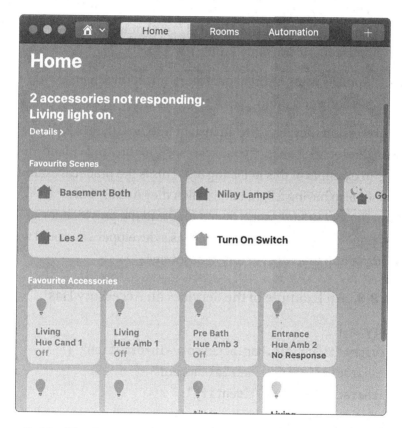

Figure 8-10. *The Home app on the Mac, most probably using an iOS-similar private API*

---

[16]Same procedure as every year: Hope for the next WWDC. 2020 it would be?

Cryptography and HAP

Usually, before the conclusion, I finish with On the Mac. Here I wanted you to know that Apple is seriously doing stuff to ensure your accessories can't be controlled by anyone walking down the street. In the *Designing Accessories for iOS and OS X*[17] session, they have a couple of very interesting slides that describe those very important elements.

- The Encryption Boundary is between HTTP and Transmission Control Protocol (TCP) or between HAP and Generic Attribute Profile (GATT).

- Apple is using bidirectional authentication & per-session encryption

In this session they also give an insight into how the HAP (HomeKit Accessory Protocol) speaks to your accessory/to the Apple platform. I'm showing an example of this in Listing 8-9. This is the practical example of a garage door also having a light bulb, which they usually have.

If you think your lamp stays on too long and the provider doesn't allow you to change it, if it's HomeKit enabled, as a developer you could write a pretty simple app that turns of this light sooner.

Listing 8-9. An Example of the Services an Accessory Has

```
accessory : {
    service1 : "public.hap.accessory-information" {
        characteristic : "serial-number"
        characteristic : "identify"
    }
```

---

[17]https://developer.apple.com/wwdc14/701 — Well, not sure how/if you will find it, but I'm lucky enough to have it on my hard drive. Apple took it offline, for whatever reason.

```
    service2 : "public.hap.garage-door-opener" {
        characteristic : "target-state"
        characteristic : "current-state"
        characteristic : "obstruction-detected"
    }
    service3 : "public.hap.lightbulb" {
        characteristic : "on"
    }
}
```

Conclusion

Home automation is one of the fields that will be with us in the future in a manner that a non-technical person might not get, in terms of privacy.

People will not analyze their network traffic with Wireshark[18] like you and I might do it. So they won't notice if a light bulb is sending your geo-coordinates when you register it, and sending a signal in the cloud every time you switch it on or off.

You as a software developer should work — together with Apple when they certify your hardware — to not spy on your users.

---

[18]https://wireshark.org is a widely-used network protocol analyzer.

Index

A

Access and Geolocation
  convenience *vs.*
    privacy, 21, 22
  metadata, 20, 21
AppleBot, 186
Apple TV, 191, 209
App Store review, 15–17
Artificial intelligence, 17
Assisted GPS, 40
Authentication
  Lock screen, 165
  passcode, 167
  SiriKit file, 165
  unlock, 167
Authorizations
  alerts, 3–5
  status, 6, 7

B

Bluetooth specs, 203

C

Calendar
  Mac request, 94
  maximum span, 82

models, 79
types, 80
Camera, 208
Camera-only access
  imagePickerController, 25
  info dictionary, 26, 27
  simulator, 26
  user interface, 25
  view controllers, 26
CLLocationManager, 108
CNAuthorizationStatus, 5
CNContactStore().request
    Access, 65, 153
Common API elements
  database, 11
  developer item, 13
  iCloud section, 9
  iOS services, 11
  iOS settings, 8, 9
  system request, 14, 15
Contact framework
  access, 78
  list of properties, 65, 66
  Mac, 74–77
Contact integration, 185
Contacts
  address book, 158
  asynchronous code, 153

© Manuel Carrasco Molina 2019
M. Carrasco Molina, *Karma-based API on Apple Platforms*,
https://doi.org/10.1007/978-1-4842-4291-9